CHRISTIANITY
IS CHRIST

CHRISTIANITY IS CHRIST

W. GRIFFITH THOMAS, D.D.

Introduction by CHARLES C. RYRIE
Illustrations by RON McCARTY

Keats Publishing, Inc.   New Canaan, Connecticut

CHRISTIANITY IS CHRIST

Shepherd Illustrated Classics edition published in 1981

The text was first published in 1909, a new edition published in 1948 and reprinted in 1958 by Church Book Room Press, Ltd. 7, Wine Office Court, Fleet Street, London E.C.4, England. The copy from which this Shepherd Illustrated Classics edition is re-issued was provided by Yale Divinity School Library, New Haven, Connecticut.

Library of Congress Catalog Card Number: 80-85341
ISBN: 0-87983-238-X

Printed in the United States of America

SHEPHERD ILLUSTRATED CLASSICS are published by Keats Publishing, Inc., 36 Grove Street, New Canaan, Connecticut 06840

CONTENTS

ILLUSTRATIONS

INTRODUCTION TO
THE SHEPHERD ILLUSTRATED
CLASSICS EDITION

Since its beginning Christianity has been subjected to attacks. Those attacks have usually centered on the person of its founder, Jesus Christ. The reason for that is simple: if Jesus Christ is not who He claimed to be, then Christianity falls with Him; for, as the title of the book correctly states, Christianity is Christ.

The apostle Peter said to be "always ready for a defense to every one asking you a word concerning the hope that is in you . . ." (1 Peter 3:15). The word "defense" is our English word "apologetics" which means a systematic defense of Christianity. That's what this book is all about, for it admirably sets forth a defense of the Christian faith in form and content as relevant today as when it was first written.

The book addresses the fundamental question, Is Jesus Christ God? If He is, then He is worthy of worship and trust. If not, then Christianity is not the unique religion it claims to be.

Though written in the first decade of this century, the significance of *Christianity Is Christ* has in no way been diminished by the passing of time. When it was first written the author said: "A special reason for giving prominence to this subject at the present time arises through the study of comparative religion. Christianity is now being compared with other religions in ways that were not possible even a few years ago, and this comparison inevitably leads up to the question of the Person of Christ. Men are asking some very pointed questions. Wherein lies the uniqueness of Christianity? . . . The Christian answer is Christ, the Person of Christ, the uniqueness of Christ and His work."

If the study of comparative religions in the author's day was sufficient ground for writing the book then, how much more is it reason for making it available today. We are living in a day when almost everything is being challenged. Eastern religions, various cults, numerous sects, even heterodox Christians, all clamor for a hearing for their brand of religion, each claiming that theirs is the right one. They accost people on the streets, address them through the media, and challenge them in the universities. As never before, people can shop in a veritable supermarket of religions.

Many, of course, have undertaken to defend Christianity throughout church history. What distinguishes this book?

It is concise yet complete. It is simple yet thorough. It is straightforward and sobering. It is faithful to the Bible. Indeed, almost all the biblical references come from the Gospels, so it mainly states the claims of Christ Himself. In one sense, it is a life of Christ, theologically presented. And good theology it exhibits throughout. Altogether it is a fine apologetic for the Christian faith.

William Henry Griffith Thomas (1861–1924) was an outstanding Anglican scholar and teacher who had a varied and wide ministry on both sides of the Atlantic. Converted at 17, he became active in the work of the church, was educated in London and Oxford and was ordained to the ministry. He served several parishes including a fruitful nine-year ministry at St. Paul's in London before becoming Principal of Wycliffe Hall, Oxford (1906–10). He then moved to Canada where he became Professor of Old Testament and later also of Systematic Theology at Wycliffe College, Toronto. In 1919 he moved to Philadelphia and undertook a variety of ministries which included travelling, lecturing, writing and conference speaking.

Dr. Thomas was associated with Lewis Sperry Chafer in the founding of Dallas Theological Seminary and was to have been the first professor of theology at the new school, but he died just before it opened. In preparing to write this introduction, I read Dr. Chafer's personal copy of *Christianity Is Christ*. Chafer's estimate was attested by penciled notations in the margin of the table of contents indicating that four of the chapters would make good series of messages—presumably for Chafer to use!

I was also pleased at the number of doctrinal themes covered so capably—topics like the son of God, son of man, meaning of the death of Christ, the virgin birth, and proofs of the resurrection of Christ. All are handled plainly and understandably.

Too, a warm spirit pervades the book. This is no detached presentation of facts, but a portrait of a Person whom the author obviously knows and loves and wants his readers to know. Neither is it an attempt to overpower with logic and reason, but to confront with a Person.

After setting forth the evidence, Dr. Thomas reminds his readers that "this case demands a verdict. It is no mere question of dialectic, no topic of argumentative discussion only, no matter of pure contemplation, no problem of philosophy. It is vital, essential, fundamental, and demands immediate and full attention. It claims the careful consideration of every mind, conscience, heart, and will."

It is a privilege to be able to reintroduce this book. For the Christian it will bring confirmation and worship. To give it to an inquiring friend could help him eternally.

Charles C. Ryrie
February 1981

CHAPTER I

THE FACT OF CHRIST

————————◄●►————————

CHRISTIANITY is the only religion in the world which rests on the Person of its Founder. A man can be a faithful Mohammedan without in the least concerning himself with the person of Mohammed. So also a man can be a true and faithful Buddhist without knowing anything whatever about Buddha. It is quite different with Christianity. Christianity is so inextricably bound up with Christ that our view of the Person of Christ involves and determines our view of Christianity.

The relation of Jesus Christ to Christianity differs entirely from that of all other founders towards the religions or philosophies which bear their names. Platonism, for example, may be defined as a method of philosophic thought from Plato; Mohammedanism as the belief in the revelation vouchsafed to Mohammed; Buddhism as the following of principles enunciated by Buddha. But Christianity is in essence adherence to the Person of Jesus Christ.[1]

It has also been pointed out that Christianity alone of the great religions of the world calls itself by the name of its Founder, and that while we call other religions by

---

[1] F. J. Foakes-Jackson, in *Cambridge Theological Essays*, p. 474.

1

the names of their founders, the adherents of these religions do not call themselves by these names.[1] This fact is full of very deep meaning. Does it not inevitably suggest that the connection between Christianity and Christ is so close as to be inseparable? Christianity is nothing less and can be nothing more than relationship to Christ.

The fundamental and ultimate idea and fact of Christianity is the Person of Christ. "What think ye of Christ?" is the crucial problem to-day, as it has been all through the centuries. It is a test of Christianity and of man's relation to Christianity. For nearly nineteen centuries attention has been concentrated on the Person of Christ both by His friends and by His foes. With a sure instinct both followers and opponents have realised the supreme importance of the Person of the Founder of Christianity. On the one hand, Jesus Christ has been the centre of opposition in almost every age; on the other hand, He has been the Object of worship and of the heart's devotion of all Christians. We cannot get away from this central fact; it influences our thinking; it controls our action; and it tests our entire attitude to the religion of Christ.

This question of the Person of Christ is predominant at the present time. For the last sixty years special and ever-increasing attention has been given to Jesus Christ. The various Lives of Christ written in Germany, France and England bear their unmistakable testimony to the perennial interest of the subject. The concentration of criticism on the Gospels to-day with an acuteness never before paralleled is proof that men of all schools realise the central and fundamental nature of the problem.

[1] R. E. Speer, *The Deity of Christ*, p. I.

History is being studied in order to discover what it has to say about Jesus Christ. The records of the primitive Church are being re-examined with minute care for their testimony to Him, and the comparison of what history and the Church have to say about Christ is once again being made with a view of discovering whether the two agree, or, if not, whether they can be properly related.

The historic Personality of Jesus has risen upon the consciousness of the Church with the force almost of a new revelation, the ultimate results of which still lie far in the future. It is literally true that this century is face to face with that Great Figure as no century has been since the first.[1]

It is thus no mere question of belief in this or that doctrine of the faith; nor simply an inquiry into the authenticity of this or that book of the Bible. It is the fundamental issue; is Jesus Christ God? Christians believe and are convinced that there is no real alternative between the acceptance of this view and the removal of Jesus Christ from the supreme place which He has occupied in the Christian Church through the centuries. Either He has been given a place to which He is entitled, or else He has been so entirely over-rated that His spiritual value cannot be regarded as anything more than that of an example. Jesus Christ must either be the Object of men's faith, or else merely its Model. The Christian Church has held firmly to the former belief, and is convinced that it is the only tenable position. It is not too much to say that at this point Christianity, as it has been known through the ages, stands or falls. Carlyle recognised this when he said, "Had this doctrine of

[1] D. S. Cairns, *Christianity in the Modern World*, p. 14.

the Divinity of Christ been lost, Christianity would
have vanished like a dream." So also Lecky truly re-
marks, "Christianity is not a system of morals; it is the
worship of a Person."

A special reason for giving prominence to this subject
at the present time arises through the study of comparative religion. Christianity is now being compared with
other religions in ways that were not possible even a
few years ago, and this comparison inevitably leads up
to the question of the Person of Christ. Men are asking
some very pointed questions. Wherein lies the uniqueness of Christianity? What was new in it? What did
Christianity bring into the world that had not appeared
before? The Christian answer is Christ, the Person of
Christ, the uniqueness of Christ and His work. The
controversy is therefore about facts. Christianity is a
historical religion, and as it claims to rest on Christ, it
necessarily follows that consideration of Christ is vital
to the reality and continuance of Christianity as a historical religion. For the same reason it is impossible for it
to avoid criticism and comparison with other faiths, nor
are Christians in the least degree afraid of any such
examination. The Person and Work of Christ can and
must be tried at the bar of Reason and of History, and
no Christian man can do other than welcome the fullest,
freest, and most searching examination of the Person of
the Founder of our religion.

A word seems necessary about the method to be
adopted in the present inquiry. There are two ways of
approaching the subject. We can commence with an
examination of the credibility of the Gospels as sources
of our knowledge of Christ, or we can start by giving
attention to the picture of Christ as enshrined in the
Gospels, and then proceed to draw our conclusions as

the result of the impressions thereby formed. The latter of these methods has been chosen. We deliberately avoid attempting to establish the credibility of the Gospels *before* studying the portrait of Christ contained in them. We prefer to reverse the process, because we wish to appeal first of all to those who are unwilling and perhaps unable to enter upon the intricacies of historical criticism. At the same time places will be found for the consideration of the criticism of the Gospels (ch. viii.) and the problems raised at the present day. But the method now deliberately adopted is to call attention to the picture of Christ, to obtain a definite impression of it as it stands, and then to draw conclusions as to the record in which it is found. We therefore take the Gospels as they are, and, assuming nothing as to their inspiration, we simply regard them as documents which are accepted to-day all over the world as the primary sources of our knowledge of Christ, and which have been so regarded by all men since at least A.D. 200. We thus start with the fewest possible presuppositions and assumptions, and endeavour to derive our doctrine of Christ from the record of the Gospels.

To the consideration, then, of the Person of Christ we address ourselves. That it is the most prominent feature of the Gospels is obvious to the most casual readers; that it was the substance of Christ's own teaching, the main theme of the Apostolic preaching and teaching, and the very life of all Church history, will be admitted by all, whatever may be their own view of Christ. We must endeavour to find out the reason of all this concentration of attention on Christ, and to see whether the Christian Church has been justified in giving this undoubted prominence and unique position to the Person of its Founder.

CHAPTER II

THE CHARACTER OF CHRIST

PERSONALITY is the highest thing in life. It is also the most interesting, attractive, fascinating. The study of personality surpasses almost everything in practical value. If this is so in general, it is essentially so with regard to the personality of Jesus Christ.

We therefore commence by a consideration of the picture of Jesus Christ as He is brought before us in the Gospels. Taking the Gospels just as they are, as documents intended to be regarded as records of the appearance of Jesus Christ on earth, we will endeavour to discover the impression formed of Him by His earliest disciples. What they thought of Christ may help us to right thoughts about Him. We will test Him just as we would any other human character.

One of His closest disciples has summed up his own impression of Jesus Christ in the following words: "We beheld His glory . . . full of grace and truth." These two words, "grace" and "truth," describe His personal character. By "grace" we are to understand His graciousness of soul, manner, attitude, speech, and action. We can see this very plainly in His influence on the daily

6

life of those disciples who were his constant companions. It is writ large on every page of the Gospels that He was attractive to people generally, and not least to little children. It is a fine test of personal power to observe how little children regard a man, and Jesus Christ answers this test to perfection. Grace was manifest in everything that He was and did. There never was such a life of graciousness to those around.

"Truth" is also another marked characteristic of the life of Jesus Christ. Reality was stamped on everything about Him. His life was holy, His word was true, His whole character was the embodiment of truth. There never has been a more real or genuine man than Jesus of Nazareth.

It is not only the presence but the combination of these two elements of grace and truth in Jesus Christ that call for attention. We cannot help noticing their perfect blend and their equally perfect proportion. Grace by itself might easily lead to weakness and mere sentimentality. Truth by itself might easily be expressed in rigour, sternness, severity. But when grace is strengthened by truth, and truth is mellowed by grace, we have the perfect character and the true life of man. It is the union of these opposites in Jesus Christ in perfect balance and consistency that demands our attention. Other men are only fragmentary, one-sided, biassed. He is completely balanced, perfect. Ordinary men often manifest unequally one or other of these two elements; Jesus Christ manifested them both in beautiful harmony and exquisite proportion. He embraces all the good elements which mark other men, and it is not too much to say that there is no element missing which men think desirable in the human character. Not only so, He possesses all these elements in a higher degree than any one else, and with perfect balance and proportion. There is no weakness, no exaggeration or strain, no strong and weak points, as is the case with the rest of mankind. Still more, there are certain elements and traits of character which are not found elsewhere, such as absolute humility, entire unselfishness, whole-hearted willingness to forgive, and the most beautiful and perfect holiness. Nor must we overlook the wonderful blending of contrasts which are to be seen in Jesus Christ; the combination of keenness and integrity, of caution and courage, of tenderness and severity, of sociability and aloofness. Or we may think of the elements of sorrow without moroseness, of joy without lightness, of spirituality without asceticism, of conscientiousness without morbidness, of freedom without licence, of earnestness without fanaticism.[1]

Yet again, the prominence given to passive virtues side by side with the evident presence and power of manliness is quite unlike what we find elsewhere; the elements of meekness, tenderness, patience, and kindness have a place in His character and attracted women to Him as well as men.

Have we ever thought of the peculiar position occupied by Jesus with respect to the ideals of the sexes? No man has ever dared to call Jesus, in any opprobrious sense, sexless: yet in character He stands above, and, if one may use the term, midway between the sexes—His comprehensive humanity a veritable storehouse of the ideals we associate with *both* the sexes. No woman has ever had any more difficulty than men have had in finding in Him the realised ideal. Whatever there is in men of strength, justice, and wisdom, whatever there is in woman of sensibility, purity, and insight, is in Christ

[1] See Dudden, *In Christ's Name*, p. 9.

without the conditions which hinder among us the development of contrasted virtues in one person.[1]

In particular, one feature of the character of Christ as portrayed in the Gospels has often been pointed out—the picture of His perfect youth. When this is contrasted with what is found in the Apocryphal Gospels the essential difference is at once seen. The beautiful sketch of Christ's boyhood and youth, with its perfect innocence, though without any weakness, is a fact to be pondered and explained. How, then, are we to account for this perfect blending and exquisite harmony? There is no doubt or question as to the environment of Jesus Christ; it was essentially and solely Jewish. His nation, place, home, work, were Jewish. And yet the picture of Jesus Christ in the Gospels is not a Jewish picture. There is nothing in Judaism to explain it. The records of Jewish history, whether of Christ's own day or of earlier times, to say nothing of later centuries, will be searched in vain for any Jewish picture corresponding to that of Jesus of Nazareth. We can see something of typical Jewish character in our Lord's day from a study of John the Baptist and St. Paul. Although, therefore, Jesus Christ is historical and Jewish, it is abundantly evident that He transcends the limits of Judaism.

Nor is it a Gentile picture. There is nothing in Greece or Rome to account for it. The greatest and highest personages of these countries have never revealed anything approaching the grace and truth manifested in Jesus Christ.

Nor can we account for this portrait by means of a blending of Jew and Gentile. There is nothing whatever

---

[1] Johnston Ross, *The Universality of Jesus*, p. 23.

in history to show that this would be the outcome of such a union of racial and personal characteristics. The typical blend of Jew and Gentile was seen in Alexandria in such a man as Philo.

We do not wonder, therefore, that the question asked by His contemporaries, "Whence hath this man this wisdom and these mighty works?" should be asked concerning His character by men of all ages, for there is nothing in history to account for Him.

This, then, is the first point upon which attention should be concentrated, the personal character of Jesus Christ. If it be said that such a character is accounted for by evolution, we naturally ask to be shown the factors which could produce such a result. Evolution necessarily presupposes a prior involution. You cannot evolve what is not there to evolve; and, bearing in mind that evolution, as generally understood, is the outcome of heredity and environment, we ask to be shown what there was in the heredity or in the environment of Jesus Christ to account for this "glory, full of grace and truth." His heredity and environment are known to mankind. Life in Palestine, together with the various racial and political influences that were at work, are all pretty familiar to those who have made themselves acquainted with the history of the time; and Christians can fairly demand the production of proof that Jesus Christ can be accounted for along the lines of natural evolution. As a well-known scientific authority has rightly said—

When evidence for a natural evolution of Christ, *i.e.* as He is portrayed to us in the Gospels, is looked for, none is forthcoming.[1]

[1] Henslow, *Christ No Product of Evolution*, p. 4.

Besides, if Jesus Christ was a product of evolution, how is it that no better man has since appeared, after nineteen centuries? Why should not evolution lead to a still higher type? Yet Jesus Christ continues to tower high above humanity. The acutest examination only confirms the truth of John Stuart Mill's well-known statement that Christ is "A unique Figure, not more unlike all His predecessors than all His followers."

This impression of the personal character of Jesus Christ is the first and earliest derived from a reading of the Gospels. But it is not the complete impression, and we must now take a further step. The perfect blending of grace and truth, although unique, is not absolutely conclusive proof of anything more than exceptional Manhood but as we continue to read the story of Jesus Christ in the Gospels we are soon brought face to face with a truly unique element. He is seen to be entirely without sin. This, if true, means that there has been one Man in whom the entail of sin was broken, one Man utterly different in this respect from every other human being of whom we have any historical or actual knowledge. This is a gigantic fact if it be true, and it calls for the severest scrutiny. We have a threefold witness to the sinlessness of Jesus Christ.

There is the witness of His foes. The Jews followed Him from place to place, watched Him with keen-eyed endeavour to entrap Him in word or deed. Pilate and Herod, who were incarnations of cleverness and cruelty, could find no fault in Him, and He was only condemned at last by the production of false witnesses. He Himself challenged His opponents to convict Him of sin; "Which of you convinceth Me of sin?" a challenge which was never met, although He was surrounded by ruthless hostility almost all through the period of His earthly Manhood.

Still more, there is the evidence of His friends. The cynical Frenchman said that "No man is a hero to his own valet," but this *dictum* is entirely set at nought by the story of Jesus Christ. One after another of His disciples bears the same testimony to Him. One of His earliest followers said of Him that He "did no sin, neither was guile found in His mouth." Another of them said "We beheld His glory." They lived with Him intimately for nearly three years, occupying the same house, travelling at times in the same little boat, sharing common needs, enduring common ostracism, and yet not one of them could ever point to the faintest shadow upon His character. This testimony is all the more remarkable because of its indirectness. It was only gradually that in looking back the disciples realised their Master was sinless, but they lay no stress on the fact. Perhaps this is because it seemed so perfectly in harmony with all they knew of Him.

Above all, there is the testimony of Christ's own life. We have the record of His intimate communion with His heavenly Father, with His prayers and some of His holiest and most intimate utterances. There is no trace of any defect ever being confessed by Him to God. He was ever preaching repentance to others, but never repented of sins of His own. Not a trace of repentance is found in Him, though human piety always begins at this point. He was always denouncing sin, but never confessed to any sin in Himself.

The best reason we have for believing in the sinlessness of Jesus is the fact that He allowed His dearest friends to think that He was. There is in all His talk no trace of regret or hint of compunction, or suggestion of sorrow for shortcoming, or

"Which of you accuseth Me of sin?"

slightest vestige of remorse. He taught other men to think of themselves as sinners. He asserted plainly that the human heart is evil, He told His disciples that every time they prayed they were to pray to be forgiven, but He never speaks or acts as though He Himself has the faintest consciousness of having ever done anything other than what was pleasing to God.[1]

Still more, we have in Jesus Christ a fact that is unique in the history of human life and character—a perfectly holy Man declaring His own holiness. The universal history of the highest and noblest of saints shows that the nearer they approached the infinite holiness of God the more conscious they became of their own lack of holiness, and yet in the case of Jesus Christ there is not only the absence of sin, but from time to time declarations of His own holiness and meekness. There was not a trace of that self-depreciation which in others is always associated with the highest character. This is all the more remarkable if we observe the instances in the life of Jesus Christ when He expressed indignation against His enemies. Yet there is nothing in His life for which He was sorry afterwards; no remembrance of evil ever impaired the consciousness of His fellowship with God. With every other man the expression of indignation tends to a subsequent feeling of compunction, or, at any rate, to a close examination whether there may not have been some elements of personal animosity or injustice in the expression of anger. But with Jesus Christ there was nothing of the kind. Not for a single instant did the faintest shadow come between Him and His heavenly Father. He was without sin.[2]

---

[1] C. E. Jefferson, *The Character of Jesus*, p. 225.
[2] Forrest, *The Authority of Christ*, pp. 10–25.

And that which we find so evident in the record of the Gospels has been acknowledged on every hand by those who have not accepted Jesus Christ in the Christian sense of the term. David Strauss could say that Jesus Christ had "a conscience unclouded by the memory of any sins." And John Stuart Mill wrote that "Religion cannot be said to have made a bad choice in pitching on this Man as the ideal representative and guide of humanity."

If it be asked why the Christian Church has made so much of the sinlessness of Christ, the answer is, because of its close and essential relation to human sin. Christianity as a religion is unique in its claim to deliver from sin, and this claim is based on the sinlessness of Christ. If Christ's own life had not been sinless, it is obvious that He could not be the Redeemer of mankind from sin. "Physician, heal thyself," would have a very definite personal application to Christ Himself.

Now this unique element of sinlessness in Christ has to be accounted for. It is a moral miracle. Only one Man out of the millions of human beings is proved to have been without sin. Deny the sinlessness of Christ, and His inner life becomes an insoluble enigma, and His claim to be the Saviour utterly falls; accept it, and at once we are met with the simple fact that there is nothing like it in nature, and that it must be a moral miracle. Now a moral miracle is just as real as a physical miracle, and it is for this reason that Christians call attention to the sinlessness of Jesus Christ. While sinlessness alone may not prove Deity, it assuredly argues for the credibility of the record and leads to the consideration of Christ's personal claims.

This, then, is the first point to be considered in regard to Christ. His perfect life of grace and truth and

His unique life of sinlessness call for attention and demand an adequate answer. The alternatives are Incarnation and Evolution. Reject Incarnation, and then Evolution is utterly unable to account for Christ.

If He was man only, we ask in the name of that holiness which is the life of the intelligent universe, and in the name of God with whom the interests of holiness are paramount, how it has come to pass, that of all men He alone has risen to spiritual perfection? What God did for piety and virtue on the earth at one time and in one case, God certainly could have done at other times and in other cases. If Jesus was man only, God could have raised up, in successive ages, many such living examples of sanctified humanity as He was, to correct, instruct, and quicken the world. But He did not; and the guilt of the moral condition of mankind is thus charged at once upon Him; and the real cause of the continuance of moral evil, and of the limited success of holiness and truth in the earth, is thus declared to be in God—that cause is the withholding of His merciful influences.[1]

Are we not right in saying with Bushnell that "The character of Jesus Christ forbids His possible classification with men"?

---

[1] J. Young, *The Christ of History*, p. 243.

CHAPTER III

THE CLAIM OF CHRIST

———◄●►———

JUST as a diamond has several facets, each one contributing to the beauty and attractiveness of the complete stone, so Jesus Christ can be considered in various ways, and to the question, "What think ye of Christ?" different answers can be given. Looking again at the Gospel story of His life, we are conscious of one remarkable fact that stands out on almost every page from the beginning to the close of His ministry. This is the claim that He made for Himself. It was a fivefold claim of a very far-reaching nature.

He claimed to be the Messiah of the Jews. It is well known that the Old Testament is a book of expectation, and that it closes with the expectation very largely unrealized. The Jews as a nation were ever looking forward to the coming of a great personage whom they called the Messiah. He would fulfil all their prophecies, realise all their hopes, and accomplish all their designs for themselves and for the world. Jesus Christ of Nazareth claimed to be this Messiah. During His ministry He referred to many a passage in the Old Testament, and pointed to Himself as the explanation and application of it. He took the Jewish law and claimed not only to fulfil it, but to give it a wider, fuller, and deeper meaning. "I came not to destroy, but to fulfil." It was this definite claim to be the Messiah that led in great part to the opposition shown to Him by the Jews.

He claimed to be in some way the Redeemer of Mankind. "The Son of Man is come to seek and to save that which is lost"; "The Son of Man came not to be ministered unto, but to minister, and to give His life a ransom for many." This description of men as "lost," *i.e.* helpless, useless, and in danger of future condemnation, and this statement about Himself as having come to "save" them, constitute a claim that implies uniqueness of relation to humanity.

He claimed to be the Master of Mankind. He said that He was the Lord of the Sabbath. He called for obedience from men by His definite, all-embracing command, "Follow Me." The earliest influence of Christ over His disciples was exercised quite naturally and simply, and yet the claim He made on them was absolute. But the narrative nowhere suggests that they felt it to be unwarranted. It is recorded without any explanation or justification, as though He had a natural and perfect right to make it. The words are so familiar that we are apt to fail to realise their astounding and far-reaching character. Think of what they mean. "He that loveth father or mother more than Me is not worthy of Me." "He that loseth his life for My sake shall find it." This remarkable claim to control lives and to be the supreme motive in life is surely more than human. He preached the kingdom of God, and announced Himself as the King. He claimed to alter the law in spite of the sanction of its hoary authority.

Still more, He claimed to be the Judge of Mankind.

He said that His words should judge mankind at the last day, and more than once He depicted Himself as the Judge before whom all men should be gathered to receive their reward or punishment. He claimed to sum up all the past and to decide all the future.

Above all, He claimed nothing less than the prerogatives of God. He claimed to be able to forgive sins, eliciting from His enemies a charge of blasphemy, since "Who can forgive sins but God only?" He associated Himself with God and God's work when He said, "My Father worketh hitherto, and I work." He told the Jews that all things had been delivered to Him of His Father, and because of this He invited all that laboured and were heavy laden to come to Him for rest. The words of St. Matthew xi. call for the closest possible study. "All things are delivered unto Me of My Father: and no man knoweth the Son, but the Father; neither knoweth any man the Father, save the Son, and he to whomsoever the Son will reveal Him. Come unto Me all ye that labour and are heavy laden, and I will give you rest." The fair and obvious interpretation of this statement is that Jesus Christ was conscious of a unique relation to God and a unique relation to man based thereon.

Is not this the New Testament picture of Jesus Christ? Can any one doubt as they read the four Gospels, or even the first three Gospels, that this, and nothing short of it, is the claim that Jesus Christ made for Himself as Messiah, Redeemer, Master, Judge, and God?

But we cannot stop with a general consideration of these remarkable claims; we must get behind them and endeavour to discover whether they are warranted by our Lord's personal consciousness. To claim is one thing; to justify and vindicate the claim is quite another. Character and deeds must bear the strain of this stupendous claim to be unique in relation to God and man. Now it is worthy of note that during recent years the minds of the greatest thinkers have been turning as never before to the consideration of the consciousness of Christ. "The Inner Life of Jesus" is the theme of modern books of great value issued in Germany and in England. The one aim that runs through them is the inquiry whether the consciousness of Jesus Christ can bear the weight of the tremendous claim which the Gospels show He made for Himself. The writers realise that the consciousness of Christ is the foundation of these claims, and that if that is wanting, the claims themselves are baseless. It is, therefore, with a sure instinct and insight that men have been giving attention to the consciousness of Christ, examining it, testing it, and proving it to the utmost. The more it is studied the better, for the more fully it is examined the more thoroughly will it be found to stand the test.

Now there is one way in particular in which this consciousness may be tested. It may be studied by dwelling on the distinctive titles that He used and allowed to be used for Himself. As Dr. Sanday rightly says, "The problem still turns round the use of those old names, Son of Man, Son of God, Messiah."[1]

"Son of Man" is a title found eighty times in the Gospels, sixty-nine in the Synoptics, and eleven in the fourth Gospel. It is found in every document into which criticism divides our present Gospels.[2] While its origin is variously explained, its meaning on our Lord's lips is not difficult of apprehension. It is employed by Ezekiel as a designation of himself, some ninety times; it is used occasionally in the Psalms of man in general (*e.g.* Psa.

---

[1] Sanday, *Life of Christ in Recent Research*, p. 123.
[2] Sanday, *op. cit.*, p. 125.

viii. 4; lxxx. 17); and it is found in a well-known passage in Daniel (ch. vii. 13) with an eschatological reference to the Messiah. It is also in Enoch and 2nd Esdras, if the passages are pre-Christian. But it does not seem to have been used by the Jews for the Messiah before Christ came, and in the New Testament, with two exceptions, it is only found on the lips of Christ Himself. The Evangelists never use it to describe their Master. It was His own designation of Himself as Messiah, and was probably derived partly from the Old Testament and partly from His own consciousness. There is ample material in the Old Testament for the germ from which it sprang, and, as Dr. Sanday says, our Lord invariably added to and deepened every Old Testament conception that He adopted.[1] It seems to suggest at once His lowliness and His Lordship, His oneness with humanity, and His uniqueness in humanity. He is the real, representative, typical Man, and the term is practically equivalent to Messiah, though it was not recognised as such in our Lord's time. The usage of the term in the Gospels may be said to fall into the two groups corresponding with the Old Testament representations of the Messiah, His lowliness as the Servant of Jehovah, and His Lordship as God's Viceregent. These two lines of Old Testament prophecy and anticipation never meet in the Old Testament itself, and it is only in Jesus Christ that the problem of their remarkable contrast is resolved and explained. While, therefore, Jesus Christ generally avoided the term "Messiah" because of the false ideas associated with it by the Jews, He found in the designation "Son of Man" a true explanation of His own Messianic consciousness and mission which it at once

---

[1] Sanday, *Life of Christ in Recent Research*, p. 127.

asserted and concealed. Thus, as Holtzmann says, "It was a riddle to those who heard it, and served to veil, not to reveal, His Messiahship."[1]

"Son of God" is another title closely related to the former. Each implies and explains the other. Its usage is not large in the Gospels. While in the Synoptics there is no explicit use of the title by Christ Himself, He employs it by implication, and certainly allows others to use it of Him. He speaks of God as "the Father" many times, but in regard to His relation to God He never associates Himself with men. Not once do we find Him speaking of "Our Father" as including Himself; it is always "My Father" and "your Father." In the same way He is never found praying *with* His disciples, though He does praise with them (St. Mark xiv. 26). Surely there is something like uniqueness here. The title "Son of God" is given to Him under a great variety of circumstances, and doubtless with a great variety of meaning, but a careful study of a number of passages compels the conclusion that, amid all the differences of circumstance and meaning, "an essential filial relation to God" is the only true interpretation (Matt. xi. 27; xvi. 16; xvii. 25; xxii. 41–45; xxvii. 43; Luke x. 22).[2] In the fourth Gospel we have one hundred and four instances of Christ calling God "Father" or "the Father," and the title "Son of God" is frequently employed, both by Himself and others (ch. i. 14–18; iii. 16–18; xx. 17). The usage is therefore clear and outstanding, and calls for explanation.

What then, does it mean? The term is found in the Old Testament as applied to Israel (Exod. iv. 22), and

[1] Quoted by Sheraton, *Princeton Theological Review*, October 1903.
[2] See Fairbairn, *Studies in the Life of Christ*, p. 193.

to the Kings of Israel (Psa. lxxxix. 26, 27), and in the second Psalm in particular a Messianic application also seems clear (ver. 7). But while it undoubtedly has an official sense, it is obvious from the usage in the Gospel that it meant very much more. The Messianic meaning was the basis of an ethical and metaphysical idea that went far beyond anything purely official (St. John v. 18; x. 33; xix. 7). The Jews clearly realised the difference between their own idea of the Sonship of the Messiah and that which Jesus claimed for Himself.

This witness of the Gospels to a unique Divine Sonship is a fact to be pondered and explained. It is impossible to avoid the force and variety of their testimony on this point.

> Copious as it is, the language . . . is all the development of a single idea. It all grows out of the *filial relation*; it is a working-out of the implications of the title Son of God. The idea, as we have seen, rests upon evidence that is far older than the fourth Gospel. It would not be wrong to call it the first proposition of Christian theology, the first product of reflection upon the Life of Christ that has come down to us. The most detailed analysis of the idea is no doubt to be found in the fourth Gospel; but that Gospel really adds nothing fundamentally new. When once we assume that our Lord Jesus Christ thought of Himself as Son, thought of Himself as *the* Son, thought of God as in a peculiar sense *His* Father, or *the* Father, all the essential data are before us.[1]

That Jesus believed Himself to be the Messiah is another fact that emerges from a careful reading of the Gospels. At the baptism it is evident that Jesus Christ was conscious of His Messiahship (Matt. iii. 15). The name Messiah was frequently applied to Jesus Christ by others. There are three occasions on which He accepted

---

[1] Sanday, *The Life of Christ in Recent Research*, p. 137.

it for Himself (Matt. xvi. 17; Mark xiv. 61–62; John iv. 26). And although He refused from time to time to reveal Himself to the Jews, who were only too ready to mistake His words and oppose His claim, the evidence of the Gospels is far too weighty to allow of any denial of the Messiahship of Jesus Christ as claimed, allowed, and implied by Him.

Some critics have called in question the fact that Jesus called Himself Messiah. But this article of evangelical tradition seems to me to stand the test of the most minute investigation.[1]

Historically considered, the calling which Jesus embraced, and with which was bound up His significance for the world, was and could be no other than to be the Messiah of His people.[2]

As Dr. Sanday truly says—

There is no explaining away this deep-rooted element in the consciousness of our Lord. On this rock the persistent efforts to minimise the significance of His Person must assuredly be shipwrecked.[3]

On these three titles, therefore, and all that they express and imply, we can concentrate attention. When they are considered, first separately, and then together in their mutual relations, they surely carry their own message as to the claim and consciousness of Christ in regard to Himself, His Father, and His Mission. They reveal to us what Dr. Sanday has so well called

Those little indications—for they are really little indications, strangely delicate and unobtrusive—scattered over the Gospels, that in spite of the humble form of His coming He

---

[1] Harnack, *History of Dogma*, i, p. 63 n.
[2] Weiss, *Life of Christ*, i, p. 195.
[3] Sanday, *op. cit.*, p. 136.

was yet essentially more than man. Let me ask you to observe how it is all in keeping. It is in keeping with what I have already called the period of "occultation." Everything about the Manhood of our Lord is (so to speak) in this subdued key. But this is only for a time. It expresses the surface consciousness, not the deeper consciousness; the deeper consciousness, after all, is expressed by St. John's "I and My Father are one." It is the unclouded openness of the mind of the Son to the mind of the Father that was the essence of His being. It is not only openness to influence, but a profound, unshakable inner sense of harmony, and indeed unity, of will. This is the fundamental fact that lies behind all our theologisings. They are but the successive efforts to put into words, coloured, perhaps, by the different ages through which the Church has passed, what St. Thomas meant by his exclamation, "My Lord and my God."[1]

This Divine consciousness is all the more remarkable when it is considered against the background of His perfect humility. We see Him occupied with His own personality, and yet proclaiming and exemplifying meekness on every possible occasion. But, if His claims were untrue, is there not something here that is not merely egotism, but blasphemy?

It is doubly surprising to observe that these enormous pretensions were advanced by one whose special peculiarity, not only among His contemporaries, but among the remarkable men that have appeared before and since, was an almost feminine tenderness and humility. Yet so clear to Him was His own dignity and infinite importance to the human race as an objective fact with which His own opinion of Himself had nothing to do, that in the same breath in which He asserts it in the most unmeasured language, He alludes, apparently with entire unconsciousness, to His own *humility*; "*I am meek and lowly in heart.*"[2]

[1] Sanday, *The Life of Christ in Recent Research*, p. 141.
[2] Masterman, *Was Jesus Christ Divine?* p. 63.

Since, too, He claimed to bring God to man in a definite and unique way, and to bestow such grace as would transform and uplift man's life, the question naturally arises whether such an One as Jesus Christ would arouse hopes in man that He could not satisfy.

Bronson Alcott once said to Carlyle that he could honestly use the words of Jesus, "I and the Father are one." "Yes," was the crushing retort, "but Jesus got the world to believe Him."[1]

And so we have to face and explain this Divine consciousness of Christ. As Canon H. B. Ottley has truly put it, this is the "Great Dilemma," and a dilemma which takes various forms. Christ was sinless, and yet was condemned as a malefactor. He was the Truth, and yet was condemned for falsehood. He came fulfilling the law, and yet was condemned as a lawbreaker. He claimed to be a King, and yet was condemned as a traitor. He was a worker of miracles, and yet was condemned as a sorcerer. He claimed to be a forgiver of sins, and yet was condemned as an impostor. He claimed to be God, and yet was condemned as a blasphemer.[2] Was ever a human being seen like this? A Man exemplifying the passive virtues combined with unique majesty. A Man challenging attention to His sinlessness and meekness, and yet obviously sincere. A Man claiming unlimited power, and yet ever expressing His dependence on God. A Man possessed of undaunted courage, and yet characterised by exceptional meekness. A Man interested in the smallest details of individual lives, and yet conscious of possessing universal relations

---

[1] *Religion and the Modern Mind.* David Smith, "The Divinity of Jesus," p. 167.

[2] H. B. Ottley, *The Great Dilemma*, passim.

with God and man. A Man deeply impressed with the awful realities and consequences of human sin, and yet ever possessed by a sunny optimism which faced the facts and looked forward to sin's eternal destruction. A man born and educated amid narrow and narrowing Jewish tradition, and yet characterised by an originality and a universality which rises infinitely above all national and racial limits. A Man of perfect humility, absolute sincerity, entire sinlessness, and yet all the while actually asserting Himself to be humble, sincere, and sinless.

A young man who had not long left the carpenter's workshop, who at the moment He spoke was in a condition of poverty, and was associated only with those who were obscure and poor like Himself, calmly declared His sense of perfect faultlessness and of extraordinary relation to God.[1]

What are we to say in the face of these astonishing claims? How are we to reconcile this self-assertion on the one hand with that high degree of personal character and excellence which all men, friends and foes, have accorded to Jesus Christ throughout the ages? How is it that these claims which would be absolutely intolerable in any other man have been allowed and almost universally accepted in the case of Jesus Christ?

Surely there is only one conclusion to all this; the old dilemma must once more be repeated, *Aut Deus aut homo non bonus.* Either Jesus Christ is God, or else He is not a good man. "If it is not superhuman authority that speaks to us here, it is surely superhuman arrogance."[2] There

[1] Young, *The Christ of History*, p. 211.
[2] *An Appeal to Unitarians*, quoted by Bishop Gore, *The Incarnation* (Bampton Lectures), p. 238.

is no middle path, for no intermediate position has ever been found tenable. Jesus Christ is either God, or else He is utterly undeserving of our thought and regard.

We therefore find ourselves face to face with the problem how to account for the Person, life, and character of Jesus Christ of Nazareth. As it has been forcibly pointed out, the ordinary factors of life cannot possibly account for Him. Race, family, place, time, education, opportunity: these are the six ordinary factors of human life, and they can all be tested to the full and examined to the last point without any of them, or even all of them together, accounting for Jesus Christ.[1] Everything in Him is at once perfectly natural and yet manifestly supernatural. He is unique in the history of mankind. As the Bishop of Birmingham has well said—

One man of a particular race and age cannot be the standard for all men, the Judge of all men, of all ages and races, the goal of human, moral development, unless he is something more than one man among many. Such a universal Manhood challenges inquiry.[2]

This inquiry Christianity invites all men to pursue. Jesus Christ cannot be ignored. Whenever human thought has endeavoured to do this it has been found impossible. Whenever human life now tries to do so the task is soon seen to be beyond it. He must be considered. He demands the attention of all true men. The supreme question to-day, as ever, is "What think ye of Christ?"

[1] Fairbairn, *Philosophy of the Christian Religion*, pp. 311, 312.
[2] Bishop Gore, *The Incarnation*, p. 25.

CHAPTER IV

THE TEACHING OF CHRIST

——————◄•►——————

FOR several years past great emphasis has been laid on the teaching of Christ. Some of the best books of modern days are on this subject. The teaching of Jesus Christ has been examined, explored, explained, classified, and applied as never before. This is all to the good, for it leads inevitably to the consideration of the Teacher Himself.

The Gospels leave no doubt as to the impression made by Christ as "a Teacher come from God." The opening of His ministry struck the keynote: "Jesus came into Galilee, preaching the gospel of the kingdom of God," and all through those three years, preaching and teaching formed a large and essential part of His work. The effect of His teaching on His contemporaries was marked and continuous. At every stage they were impressed by Him. The "understanding and answers" which at the age of twelve astonished the teachers in the Temple gave promise of what was abundantly evident in after-years. It will help us to understand His teaching more thoroughly to-day if we first endeavour to gain an idea of how it impressed His earliest hearers. At the

28

Jesus came into Galilee, preaching the gospel of God.

opening of His ministry the people of Nazareth were astonished at the *graciousness* of His utterances (Luke iv. 22). There was a glow of grace and love, an accent of persuasiveness, a note of considerateness, a touch of tenderness in what He said that deeply impressed them. On another occasion the *authoritativeness* of His teaching was the prominent feature (Matt. vii. 29). In contrast with their own teachers, He seemed to speak from personal knowledge, and the force of His convictions awed them. In close association with this was His *boldness* (John vii. 26). Unlettered though He was, there was no timidity or self-consciousness, no hesitation as to what He felt to be truth. Without any thought of Himself or His audience, He spoke out fearlessly on every occasion, utterly heedless of the consequences to Himself, and only concerned for truth and the delivery of His Father's message. The *power* of His teachings was also deeply felt. "His word was with power" (Luke iv. 32). The spiritual force of His personality expressed itself in His utterances and held His hearers in its enthralling grasp. And so we are not surprised to read of the impression of *uniqueness* made by Him. "Never man spake like this Man" (John vii. 46). The simplicity and withal the depth, the directness and yet the universality, the charm and yet the truth of His teaching made a deep mark on His hearers, and elicited the conviction that they were in the presence of a Teacher such as man had never known before. And thus the large proportion of teaching in the Gospels, and the impressions evidently created by the Teacher Himself are such that we are not at all surprised that years afterwards the great Apostle of the Gentiles should recall these things and say, "Remember the words of the Lord Jesus" (Acts xx. 35). The same impression has been made in every age since the days of Christ and His immediate followers, and in any full consideration of His Person as the substance of Christianity great attention must necessarily be paid to His teaching.

What, then, was the substance of His teaching, which has been so attractive to the world? First and foremost, His teaching about God. Two ideas perhaps sum it up; the Kingdom of God and the Fatherhood of God. The term "Kingdom of God" is found over one hundred times in the Gospels and in every part of the ministry from the outset to the end. Its central idea is the reign and rule of God over human life, and it was the theme of Christ's preaching from the first. "The Kingdom of God" was the earliest word in Jerusalem (John iii. 3) and in Galilee (Mark i. 15), and the theme is found in sermon, parable, and prophecy to the close of His ministry. Man ruled over by God, and thereby finding the full realisation of life: this is the essence of the idea of the Kingdom of God. The Fatherhood of God is equally characteristic of Christ's teaching, and although it was known in part before, by reason of God's unique covenant relation to Israel, it came with all the force and freshness of a new revelation. While the holiness and majesty of God as emphasised in Old Testament times were presupposed and taken for granted, the thought of Fatherhood was added, giving richness and fulness to the message, and joy and hope to the hearers. This Fatherhood was essentially spiritual and ethical, and correlated with a spiritual and ethical sonship, and was proclaimed with such frequency and variety that it had all the glory of a new revelation concerning God's relation to man. And so from the day of Christ we have had ideas of God, and of God in relation to man, that the world never knew before Christ came. Our highest and best knowledge, indeed almost all we know of God, has come from or through Him. The very high ideas of God which some men say are impossible of practical realisation have really come from Christ.

In close connection with Christ's teaching about God was His message of forgiveness for man. It was soon evident that He had come not only to reveal, but also to redeem. The fact of sin was therefore emphasised and the need of deliverance from it pointed out. On the paralytic brought for healing, Jesus Christ bestowed first of all the man's deepest need, forgiveness, and all through His ministry in a variety of ways sin and redemption were prominent features of His teaching. The burden of human iniquity and the bounty of Divine mercy were His themes. No wonder the "common people heard Him gladly" (Mark xii. 37), or that "sinners" flocked to Him (Luke xv. i). It was the glory of His ministry that He brought peace and rest to weary, sin-stricken hearts by His message of a free, full forgiveness. In the face of murmuring and opposition He justified His conduct by saying that "the Son of Man came to seek and to save that which was lost" (Luke xix. 10).

Arising out of this message of redemption was another closely allied to it—the value and possibility of human life when thus redeemed. "How much, then, is a man better than a sheep?" (Matt. xii. 12). This, too , may be said to have been a keynote of Christ's teaching. The possibility of redemption from sin and of becoming a child of God in ethical relationship led immediately and naturally to the great truth of the possibility of holiness and service. "Born again," and within the Kingdom of God (John iii. 3, 5), the redeemed soul can grow and expand, and deepen into untold capabilities of character, conduct, and usefulness. As no heart was too hard for His mercy, so no life was too poor for His grace. There was hope for the worst and encouragement for the feeblest through the infinite possibilities of Divine love and grace. These three great truths concerning God, forgiveness, and human life, expressing as they do the three ideas of Revelation, Redemption, and Restoration, may be said to summarise and include all the important and essential elements of Christ's teaching. While He never taught systematically, there are certain "ruling ideas"[1] which may be regarded as the cardinal points of His message. He came to bring God to men and to bring men to God: this sums up all His teaching.

If the substance of Christ's teaching is noteworthy, so also are its characteristics. Not only the immediate hearers but readers of the Gospels in all ages have been attracted and impressed by the way in which the teaching was given. Other religions have had their ethical ideals of duty, opportunity, and even of love, but nowhere have they approached those of Christ either in reality or in attractiveness or in power. Christ's message is remarkable for its *universal adaptation*. Its appeal is universal; it is adapted to all men from the adult down to the child; it makes its appeal to all times, and not merely to the age in which it was first given. And the reason of this is that it emphasises a threefold ethical attitude towards God and man which makes a universal appeal as nothing else does or perhaps can do. Christ calls for repentance, trust, and love. Repentance in relation to Sin; Trust in relation to God; and Love in relation to God and man. Nowhere else do we find this specific appeal. The universal obligation of Repentance,

[1] D'Arcy, *Ruling Ideas of Our Lord*, Preface.

Trust, and Love is the peculiar contribution of Christianity to the ethics of the world.

The *completeness* of Christ's teaching is also to be observed. It touches life at every point, from the regulation of the thoughts and motives to the control of the will and conduct. Its moral ideal is love to God and man, and in this is a unity which binds in one all the elements of the spiritual life. Its emphasis on humility and its exclusion of fame and reputation, its refusal to pander to any personal interest, its insistence on the passive virtues, thereby practically adding an entirely new realm of morality—all show the completeness of Christ's ethic. Nor can we fail to see this also in the fact that since the days of Christ, in spite of all the progress of thought, not a single new ethical idea or ideal has been given to the world.

The *inexhaustibleness* of the teaching of Christ is constantly being realised. Generation after generation finds in it what is new, fresh, and inspiring. Christ said, "Heaven and earth shall pass away, but My words shall not pass away" (Matt. xxiv. 35), and every day brings fresh proof of the truth of this statement.

Never did the Speaker seem to stand more utterly alone than when He uttered this majestic utterance. Never did it seem more improbable that it should be fulfilled. But as we look across the centuries we see how it has been realised. His words have passed into laws, they have passed into doctrines, they have passed into proverbs, they have passed into consolations, but they have never "passed away." What human teacher ever dared to claim an eternity for his words?[1]

From this it follows that Christ's teaching has a *permanence* all its own. It is not discarded and set aside as

---

[1] Maclear, *St. Mark*, The Cambridge Bible for Schools, p. 149.

obsolete even by the greatest thinkers of the world. Christ's teaching is almost as remarkable for what it omits as for what it includes.

One of the strongest pieces of objective evidence in favour of Christianity is not sufficiently enforced by apologists. Indeed I am not aware that I have ever seen it mentioned. It is the absence from the biography of Christ of any doctrines which the subsequent growth of human knowledge—whether in natural science, ethics, political economy or elsewhere—has had to discount. This negative argument is really almost as strong as is the positive one from what Christ did teach. For when we consider what a large number of sayings are recorded of—or at least attributed to—Him, it becomes most remarkable that in literal truth there is no reason why any of His words should ever pass away to the point of becoming obsolete. . . . Contrast Jesus Christ in this respect with other thinkers of like antiquity. Even Plato, who, though some four hundred years before Christ in point of time, was greatly in advance of Him in respect of philosophic thought, is nowhere in this respect as compared with Christ. Read the Dialogues, and see how enormous is the contrast with the Gospels in respect of errors of all kinds, reaching even to absurdity in respect of reason, and to sayings shocking to the moral sense. Yet this is confessedly the highest level of human reason on the lines of spirituality when unaided by alleged revelation.[1]

From all this it is not surprising, therefore, to observe the *authoritativeness* of Christ's teaching. Both in His earthly ministry and ever since, men have realised that He speaks "with authority," and that His words are final. There is a sureness, an absence of doubt and hesitation about what He says; He does not recall or modify, or safeguard, or add. Within the limits of His sphere there is no correction, and while whole continents of knowledge were outside His plan, there was no

[1] G. J. Romanes, *Thoughts on Religion*, p. 157.

indication of error in what He actually said. While His knowledge was limited by the conditions and requirements of His earthly manifestation, it was infallible within those limitations. His words carried conviction even in the face of opposition. Although He was denied and rejected, yet He could not be gainsaid; it was so evident that He lived all He taught.

That sinless consciousness is the fountain-head of our faith and our morals. We can no more get beyond Jesus than we can sail past the North Star. Whole chapters of *Aristotle* are out of date. Some sections of *Paradise Lost* now seem unworthy of the writer and unmeaning to the reader. But just as the sense of beauty culminated in Greece some twenty-three centuries ago, so that all our artists bend in admiration over a poor fragment of the Elgin marbles, so the revelation of ethical standards culminated in Palestine. The Parthenon, battered and crumbling, shows us a building beyond which architecture may not go. We may build something different—something more nearly perfect no man hopes to build. So character reached its supreme embodiment and standard in Jesus of Nazareth. We desire no new edition of the Sermon on the Mount, and no modification of the Golden Rule. We can easily surpass Jesus in the length of His life, or the quantity of His labour, or in the amount of His human knowledge. In quality and revealing power He is unsurpassable and final. Different men there may be and should be; but in the realm of character and religion a greater master and leader the world will never see.[1]

Not least of all these characteristics is the *verifiableness* of Christ's teaching. He who "wills to do His will shall know of the doctrine" (John vii. 17). It is a thing which verifies itself in human lives because it possesses a dynamic, a special and unique power for making itself a force in the hearts of men. It introduces into morality

---

[1] W. H. P. Faunce, *The Educational Ideal in the Ministry*, p. 33.

an entirely new spirit, the filial spirit, the joyous response of a child to a Father. No longer merely under obligation to an impersonal law, the disciple of Christ realises, is conscious of, and obedient to, the will of a loving Father. Love to Christ is the response of the soul, and

It is the only thing in the region of moral motives that can be described as an imperishable yet convertible force, whose changes of form never mean decrease of energy or loss of power.[1]

No wonder, then, that the original hearers of Christ were impressed by the "charm" ($\chi \acute{\alpha} \varrho \iota \varsigma$) of His words, or that succeeding ages should have pondered His words and placed them high above all others as the supreme and final word in ethics.

Some years since Sir Edwin Arnold, the distinguished poet, and author of *The Light of Asia*, and Dr. William Ashmore of China, the heroic and renowned American missionary, met each other on a Pacific steamship. "I have been criticised," said Sir Edwin Arnold to Dr. Ashmore, "for an implied comparison between Buddhism and Christianity in regard to the doctrines derived from them and the principles contained in them respectively. No such object was in my mind. For me, Christianity, rightly viewed, is the crowned queen of religions, and immensely superior to every other; and though I am so great an admirer of much that is great in Hindu philosophy and religion, I would not give away one verse of the Sermon on the Mount for twenty epic poems like the Mahabharata, nor exchange the Golden Rule for twenty new Upanishads."[2]

---

[1] Fairbairn, *Christ in Modern Theology*, p. 380.
[2] Hoyt, *The Lord's Teaching Concerning His Own Person*, p. 42. See also a fine passage in A. C. Benson's *The House of Quiet*, p. 71.

But it may be asked, it often is asked, wherein lay the originality, the uniqueness of Christ's teaching? Wherein was He so really and essentially different from other teachers that He is removed entirely out of the same category? Now it may at once be said that the fact, the admitted fact, that Christian ethic is the highest the world has ever seen is in itself no proof of its divine origin. It may be only the highest and best experienced thus far in the evolution of human thought and endeavour. Nor should it be surprising if we find in Christ's teaching much that is found elsewhere, for the simple reason that human nature and its ethical needs are practically the same under all circumstances, and it would have been impossible for Jesus to have avoided emphasising those essential features of life and duty which are common to all. Originality, therefore, is not of supreme moment.

Lotze and Harnack regard as the great point in which Christianity is unique the value it assigns to each individual man in its assertion that every man is a child of God.[1] Other points emphasised by Harnack as characteristic of Christianity as of no other religion are the severance of the existing connection between ethics and external forms of religion; the insistence on the root of morality in the intention and disposition; the concentration on the one basis and motive—love, and the combination of religion and morality in the union of love and humility. Thus the problem of accounting for Christ as a Teacher is a very real one. How are we to explain the substance and characteristics of His teaching in view of all the circumstances of His life, race, and environment?

---

[1] Lotze, *Microcosmus*, vol. ii. book 8, ch. 4, "The Religious Life." Harnack, *What Is Christianity*, pp. 63 ff., 68, 70 ff.

It is sometimes said, Everything that Jesus said had been said before Him by others. Let us grant that it is true, what then? Originality may or may not be a merit. If the truth has already been uttered, the merit lies in repeating it, and giving it new and fuller application. But there are other considerations to be borne in mind. We have no other teacher who so completely eliminated the trivial, the temporal, the false from his system, no one who selected just the eternal and the universal, and combined them in a teaching where all these great truths found their congenial home. These parallels from the teaching of others to that of Christ are brought together from this quarter and from that; how was it that none of these teachers furnishes us with any parallel to the teaching of Christ as a whole, while each of them gives us such truths as He expresses mingled with a mass of what is trivial and absurd? How was it that a carpenter, of no special training, ignorant of the culture and learning of the Greeks, born of a people whose great teachers were narrow, sour, intolerant, pedantic legalists, was the supreme religious Teacher the world has known, whose supremacy here makes Him the most important figure in the world's history?[1]

But the real newness of Christ as a Teacher is found in His Person rather than in what He said or in the way He said it. The unique contribution Christ makes to ethics is Himself. It is the way in which He associates His teaching with Himself that demands and commands attention. He connects the Kingdom of God with Himself as King. He links the Fatherhood of God with Himself as the unique Revealer (Matt. xi. 27). He associates Forgiveness with His own prerogative and authority (Mark ii. 10). He teaches the value and possibilities of human life in intimate connection with Himself as its Master here and its Judge hereafter. There is no word of His teaching which He does not in some way make to depend on Himself.

[1] Peake, *Christianity: Its Nature and Its Truth*, pp. 226 f.

We can see this in the Gospels at every stage from the first to the last. His teaching is a revelation of Himself. His ministry was marked off into three great periods, in each of which He was occupied mainly and predominantly with one particular subject. Not that these are absolutely distinguished or that they do not overlap, but they are defined with sufficient clearness to allow of our observing the great theme of each period. His ministry commenced with the preaching of the Kingdom of God (Matt. iv. 17, ἀπὸ τότε). In this period Christ was essentially and pre-eminently the Prophet. The Sermon on the Mount, the Parables, and other teaching were all concentrated on the Kingdom. This part of the ministry culminated in the confession of St. Peter at Cæsarea Philippi. At that time and thenceforward we observe a marked change (Matt. xvi. 21, ἀπὸ τότε), and the main subject of His teaching was His approaching suffering and death. In a variety of ways this theme was uppermost until a few days before His death. It may be said to culminate in the incident associated with the desire of the Greeks to see Christ (John xii. 21). These references to His atoning death naturally associate themselves with the idea of Jesus as a Priest and Sacrifice. Then from the triumphal entry on Palm Sunday we are at once conscious of yet another change, and He appears before the people and before His disciples in a new guise. The entry itself with its publicity was quite different from His former attitude of secrecy. His teaching began to refer to the future, and became largely eschatological. Parables of judgment and predictions of His own coming stood out prominently in the teaching of that week, and in all this Jesus Himself assumes the attitude of King and Judge. There is nothing more striking in the Gospels than this royal and judicial element in the events and teaching of the closing days of His earthly life.

And thus His teaching all through the Gospels is summed up in His mission, and this is threefold. In the language of theology, He came to be Prophet, Priest, and King. As Prophet He reveals God to man; as Priest He redeems man for God; as King He rules and judges mankind. Revelation, Redemption, Rule—these constitute His mission, and each point is found in His teaching. He interprets God to man, He brings man to God and God to man, and He exercises Divine authority in relation to man. For the spiritual life of man these three offices meet three human needs, spiritual illumination, redemption, and government. In the Old Testament these offices were never blended in one person; there were separate prophets, priests, and kings, but in Christ they met for the first time and blended, and in this completeness of Divine provision man's life is satisfied and blessed. Hence it is not so much in the ideas of Christianity that its superiority is seen, as in the dynamic for realising them, a dynamic found in the relation of the soul to Christ and to those who are in like manner associated with Christ in a society of His followers.

Now it is this association, definite, intimate, and essential, between Christ's teaching and Himself that constitutes the real problem. He Himself is the real theme of His teaching. This is certainly a unique feature among the teachers of the world. A true teacher usually keeps himself in the background and makes his message prominent. But here Jesus Christ is Himself the Truth, and is at once the Subject of His teaching and the Medium through whom Truth is to be perceived and received.

His words were so completely parts and utterances of Himself, that they had no meaning as abstract statements of truth uttered by Him as a Divine oracle or prophet. Take away Himself as the primary (though not the ultimate) subject of every statement and they all fall to pieces.[1]

This is the absolutely unique contribution of Christ to ethics, Himself. There is scarcely a passage in the Gospels without the self-assertion of Jesus coming out in connection with His teaching. His message and His claims are really inextricable. We have already seen what this self-assertion means in general (ch. iii.), but one element may be specially emphasised here in connection with His teaching. In His eschatological teaching Jesus repeatedly refers to Himself as Judge of the world. Do we realise what this means and involves? A young Jewish carpenter claims to be the judge of all mankind!

The place assigned in the last judgment to Himself in the words of Jesus is recognised by all interpreters to imply that the ultimate fate of men is to be determined by their relation to Him. He is the standard by which all shall be measured; and it is to Him as the Saviour that all who enter into eternal life will owe their felicity. But the description of Himself as Judge implies much more than this: it implies the consciousness of ability to estimate the deeds of men so exactly as to determine with unerring justice their everlasting state. How far beyond the reach of mere human nature such a claim is, it is easy to see.[2]

This simple but all-significant fact of the connection between the Person and the teaching, which is patent to every reader of the Gospels, has been felt ever since the

---

[1] Hort, *The Way, the Truth, and the Life*, p. 207.
[2] Stalker, *The Christology of Jesus*, p. 241.

days of Christ. Just as the Jews opposed Him because He made Himself equal with God, because His teaching implied and involved immense claims for Himself, so men have never been able to rest long in His teaching alone; it has inevitably led them up to His personality and compelled them to face His claims. Besides, ideas alone never save and inspire lives; they must have a personality behind to give them reality, vitality, and dynamic. A disciple is more than a scholar, and inspiration is more than instruction. Christ's words are of permanent value because of His Person; they endure because He endures.

The egoism of all this has to be reckoned with much more seriously than is sometimes done by men who profess to accept Jesus as Teacher while denying him as Lord. The self-assertion of Christ is either a serious blot on His character or an integral part of a gracious and deliberate saving purpose of God.[1]

It is simply impossible to accept the teachings without acknowledging the claim of the Teacher. So inextricably are they bound up that men in sacrificing the one are not long before they let the other go also. It is an utterly illogical and impossible position for any one to accept the Sermon on the Mount without recognising the full claims of Christ as Master and Judge which He made in that discourse.

It will in the long run, I believe, be found impossible to maintain supreme reverence for the character of Jesus, and to reject the truth of His ideas. The character is simply the ideas translated into temper and conduct. If the ideas are illusory, then the character is not in accordance with the nature of things, and in such a case it is not what we ought to imitate

[1] Johnston Ross, *The Universality of Jesus*, p. 122.

or admire. All such admiration is simply sentimentality; it is not ethical, and it stands in the way of human progress. But if we cannot face this, if we feel, in spite of ourselves, awe and veneration for the character of Jesus, we must, sooner or later, go on to faith in the ideas.[1]

Christianity in its final and ultimate analysis is the acceptance of the Person not the teaching of Christ. He came not so much to teach as to redeem, and redemption involves His Person, His community of believing followers, His relation to and rule over their lives. As Dr. R. W. Dale used to say, Jesus Christ came not to preach the Gospel, but that there might be a Gospel to preach. And it is the Gospel which He Himself *is* rather than anything He ever taught that constitutes Christianity. What think ye of the teaching? is an interesting, valuable inquiry. But, What think ye of the Teacher? is far more important, and more vital and central to the issues involved in the problem before us.

[1] Cairns, *Christianity in the Modern World*, p. 19.

CHAPTER V

THE MIRACLES OF CHRIST

———◆◆——

FOR our present purpose of answering the question "What think ye of Christ?" it is necessary and important to observe the place given to our Lord's miracles in the Gospels. A careful study of them, just as they appear, reveals the undoubted fact that they were not wrought by our Lord primarily for evidential purposes, for convincing those who were not as yet His disciples. At the outset of His ministry we are significantly told of the limited result of His first miracle. "This beginning of miracles did Jesus in Cana of Galilee, and manifested forth His glory; and His disciples believed on Him" (John ii. 11). "His disciples"—that was all; no one else of the company seems to have been impressed. Soon afterwards, when He exercised His authority by cleansing the Temple of the money-changers, He was asked to justify His action by means of a miracle. "What sign shewest Thou unto us, seeing that Thou doest these things?" Instead of working a miracle, He referred them to the then far-off event of His resurrection. "Destroy this Temple, and in three days I will raise it up." In the same way throughout His ministry He frequently enjoined silence on those on whom He had bestowed physical blessing, a silence which would have been unnecessary, out of place, and inexplicable if the primary idea of miracles had been to spread the knowledge of Himself over the land. Of course it was inevitable that such works should become known and have their effect in calling attention to Him, but this was a consequence rather than the primary purpose. The same secondary place of miracles is seen in our Lord's words to His disciples on the eve of His passion. He puts first, belief in Himself apart from miracles. "Believe Me that I am in the Father" (John xiv. II). And then He introduces miracles only if the disciples could not other-wise rise to faith in Him. "Or else believe Me for the very works' sake" (ver. II). In accordance with this, the summary statement of the purpose of the Fourth Gospel is significant. "Many other signs truly did Jesus in the presence of *His disciples*" (John xx. 30). Another indication in the same direction are the words used to describe these wonderful works. The first in order of thought is τέφας, *wonder*, which expresses the feelings of the witnesses in the presence of what had been done. The next is δυνάμις, *power*, which indicates the result of their thought as it began to play on these deeds; some "power" was evidently at work. But the most important of all is σημεῖον, *sign*, which clearly indicates the place of miracles in the Gospels. They were signs of something other and higher than themselves—they were symbolical of Christ's Divine mission. But it should be observed that a "sign" is not necessarily a proof, and it is significant that the miracles are never called by any word meaning "proof." The word "proof" (τεκμήφιον, Acts i. 3) is only found in connection with our Lord's manifestation of Himself after His resurrection. In other words, the great proof was

Himself rather than His works. A sign cannot compel belief, or enemies would surely have been convinced. It only carries a meaning, or *sign*, or significance to those who are already impressed. So Westcott rightly says that—

> Miracles or signs are more properly in their highest form the substance than the proofs of revelation. . . . The best idea which we can form of a miracle is that of an event or phenomenon which is fitted to suggest to us the action of a personal spiritual power. . . . Its essence lies not so much in what it is in itself as in what it is calculated to indicate.[1]

We may observe this true place of miracles still further as we contemplate the almost utter disregard of them on the part of those in whose presence they were wrought. They created interest and stirred curiosity, but apparently they seldom led to conviction unless there had been some other predisposing cause of faith in Christ. The powerlessness of miracles to convince the gainsayer is clearly seen in the words, "When Christ cometh, will He do more miracles than this man doeth?" (John vii. 31). "Though He had done so many miracles before them, yet they believed not on Him" (John xii. 37). Those who were not prepared to receive His message without miracles were not as a rule ready to accept miracles as an attestation of His Divine commission.

The phenomenon, I say, which is apprehended as a miracle suggests the idea of the action of a personal spiritual power. But in itself it can do no more than suggest the idea of his action. It is wholly unable in any intelligible sense to prove the existence of such a power, and still less to prove that the power is Infinite.[2]

---

[1] Westcott, *The Gospel of Life*, p. 76.
[2] Westcott, *op. cit.*, p. 76.

In view of this clear indication of the place of miracles and purpose of miracles in the life of Christ it is obvious that we cannot, and, indeed, for our present purpose we have no need to emphasise them as evidences for His Person. Any such evidence that they carried was to contemporaries only, and this necessarily diminishes in force with lapse of time.

Few would now maintain that the miracles are *to us* proofs of the Divine mission of Jesus Christ. Their evidential force, supposing them to have been wrought, was immediate: they appealed to those who originally saw them. And the conviction aroused in the primary witnesses could not be communicated to later generations. Thus the problem presented by our Lord's miracles is for us less theological and apologetic and far more historical and literary than it used to appear to our fathers.[1]

For us to-day the Person of Christ is the great miracle, and the true line of thought is to argue from Christ to miracles rather than from miracles to Christ.

We are not then justified, either by reason or by Scripture, in assigning to miracles, and still less to the record of miracles, a supreme power of proof. But none the less they fulfil externally an important function in the Divine economy. They are fitted to awaken, to arouse, to arrest the faith which is latent. They bring men who already believe in God into His presence. They place them in an attitude of reverent expectation.[2]

But this is not for an instant to say that the miraculous element in the Gospels is not a fitting and even necessary part of the record of the life of Christ. On the contrary, the place of the miracles in the Gospels is

[1] Bishop Chase, *Cambridge Theological Essays*, p. 402. See also Illingworth, *Divine Immanence*, pp. 88–90.
[2] Westcott, *The Gospel of Life*, p. 82.

exactly what we should have expected from One whose Person was what His was.

Since Jesus was verily an incarnation of the Godhead, miraculous works in His life were only becoming and natural. This does not in the least exclude the application of the severest criticism to the historical accounts of the Christian miracles. But the unbroken course of nature, in the presence of a fact so stupendous as Incarnation, had been of all things unnatural and incredible.[1]

It is the most natural and obvious thing in the world that He who was what He was should do what the Gospels record of Him. And it is noteworthy that one of the words very frequently used of these miracles in the Gospels is the ordinary term, works (εργα). They were the natural and necessary outcome of His life, the expression in act of what He Himself was.

The moral elevation and religious intensity of the Gospels should count for something. The indissoluble connexion between the works and the words of Jesus, between these and His character and consciousness, must receive due regard. The narratives of miracles are woven into the very texture of the evangelical record. How many of the sayings of Jesus are closely linked with works of healing? How many of the most beautiful and attractive traits in the portrait of Jesus are drawn from His dealing with sufferers who came to Him for relief?[2]

That His own abundant vitality should have been somehow communicated to other persons is not surprising. That One who was so full of life and compassion should seek to help and bless the needy was surely to be expected.

---

[1] Young, *The Christ of History*, p. 255.
[2] Garvie, *Studies in the Inner Life of Jesus*, p. 51.

The miracles are harmonious with the character and consciousness of Jesus; they are not external confirmations, but internal constituents of the revelation of the Heavenly Father's love, mercy, and grace, given in Him, the beloved Son of God, and the compassionate Brother of men.[1]

The miracles were not merely marvels; with two exceptions (which are not sufficient to set aside the general principle) they were restorative and beneficent.

The motive and scope of the Lord's miracles recorded in the Gospels are ever the same. The notices of the miracles are scattered up and down over the Gospels. But when they are considered in relation to each other, we discover in them an undesigned unity. Together they cover the whole ground of our Lord's work as the Saviour, renewing each element in man's complex being and restoring peace in the physical order. They are not presented in the Gospels as primarily designed to enhance His dignity and His power. If they had been the invention of pious fancy, yearning to illustrate by imposing stories His greatness and His glory, it is a moral impossibility that this subtle unity of purpose should have been so consistently and so unobtrusively observed.[2]

We are therefore not now concerned with the abstract problem of the possibility of the miraculous; such a question would be entirely unnecessary for our present purpose. We are face to face with a supernatural Person, and the question whether He could or did do supernatural works is after all not of the first importance. The supreme question is as to the Person Himself, for "a sinless Christ is as great a miracle as a Christ who can walk on the water."[3] The question of miracles has often been too widely separated from the question

---

[1] Garvie, *op. cit.*, p. 51.

[2] Chase, *Cambridge Theological Essays*, p. 404.

[3] Bruce, *Humiliation of Christ*, p. 208, note I.

of the miraculous Person. Modern thought in its belief in the uniformity of nature has undoubtedly modified our conception of the supernatural, and the "supernatural is not for us the same thing as the arbitrary or unnatural."[1] But the demand for absolute regularity of nature would really exclude Christ Himself as supernatural, and also make His appearance in time nothing more than the outcome of natural evolutionary processes. We therefore really gain nothing by simply insisting on absolute uniformity of nature as the great modern law, unless we are prepared to go further and deny the possibility of any Divine interposition which, while being not "arbitrary or unnatural" should nevertheless be truly supernatural.

Every one will concede to Dr. Sanday "the uniformity of the *ordinary* course of nature." If it were otherwise, we should have no world in which we could live at all. The question is not, Do natural causes operate uniformly? but, Are natural causes the only causes that exist or operate? For miracle, as has frequently been pointed out, is precisely the assertion of the interposition of a *new* cause; one, besides, which the theist must admit to be a *vera causa*.[2]

If, therefore, we are to allow the scientific doctrine of the uniformity and continuity of nature to bar the way, we shall inevitably come to the conclusion that miracles are impossible, and from this would follow, as it usually does follow, the conclusion that a miraculous Christ is impossible. The question is thus really decided on *a priori* grounds before the evidence is even looked at.

But how, then, is the modern position to be met? How are we to retain our belief in the uniformity of nature and also in the miracles? In one way only: by

[1] Sanday, *Expository Times*, vol. xx, p. 158.
[2] Orr, *The Resurrection of Jesus*, p. 51.

predicating a true theistic view of the world. To the materialist miracle is, of course, impossible, but on the assumption that God is, and is at once transcendent and immanent, miracles are not impossible.

Those who accept the evangelical narratives of miracles do not assume any breach in the continuity of nature, any disregard of the universal laws of movement . . . Negatively, we define miracles as events which nature as known in our common experience cannot explain . . . Positively, we define miracles as events which, because of their character and purpose, we ascribe to the will of God, being ignorant whether that will acts directly or uses means of which we know nothing . . . May not that Divine will act generally according to fixed habit, and yet for special ends act in a way new and strange? In life physical forces are transcended; so are vital processes in mind; the process of evolution allows at this stage or that a Divine initiative. Grant the moral significance and religious value of Jesus, is it incredible or unreasonable to hold that such a Divine initiative is connected with His Person?[1]

The Person of Christ is therefore a great miracle, and the issue cannot be evaded. He represents a definite, Divine intervention on behalf of man at a particular moment of time in the world's history, and on this great miracle of the Person of Christ we take our stand.

Jesus, in a word, was Deity manifested in humanity and under the conditions of time. Now this is in itself an extraordinary conception, and it is made more extraordinary by the marvellous way in which it is embodied in a personal history. There never was a loftier idea, or one better calculated to challenge prompt and complete contradiction, than the one expressed in our Gospels, models though they be of simplicity in narrative and language. Their common purpose is to describe the life and record the words of a person they

[1] Garvie, *Studies in the Inner Life of Jesus*, p. 52.

conceive as miraculous. . . . What is common to all four Evangelists, and what is in their mind essential, is the idea, not that the miraculous history proves the person to be supernatural, but that the history was miraculous because it articulated and manifested the supernatural person. The Gospels may indeed be described as the interpretation of this person in the terms of history; and so regarded, the Jesus of Mark is as miraculous as the Jesus of John.[1]

When this is clearly seen the question of the number and character of the miracles becomes quite secondary. The inquiry resolves itself simply into this: granted such a supernatural Person, were supernatural deeds congruous with His life? The character of the works attributed to Him, their beneficence, the restraint under which they were worked, the comparatively insignificant place they occupied in His ministry, and the constant stress laid by Him on spiritual kinship as primary— these are all entirely congruous with the manifestation and working of so miraculous and superhuman a Person as Jesus is seen to be. Two things are perfectly clear to all careful readers of the Gospels. (1) The writers do recognise a distinction between natural events and miracles, between occurrences which are ordinary and extraordinary. As Westcott says—

Whole structures of popular objections, for example, fall before a simple statement like that in which the Evangelist undesignedly contrasts the ministry of the Baptist with the ministry of Christ: "John indeed did no sign" (John x. 41).[2]

(2) The writers considered that there was an extraordinary element in our Lord's life.

---

[1] Fairbairn, *The Philosophy of the Christian Religion*, p. 326.
[2] Westcott, *The Gospel of Life*, p. 83.

That there was conspicuously present in the Lord's life an element of activity transcending common experience is a conclusion which rests on amply sufficient evidence.[1]

Nor must it be overlooked that this miraculous element is as clear and prominent in the earliest strata of the Gospels as it is in their present form. Let Mark be the earliest document, and let the irreducible minimum of that be found, and it will still be seen that miracles are its warp and woof. And this is so because behind the deeds is the miraculous Person. When we accept Him miracles become credible.

[1] Chase, *Cambridge Theological Essays*, p. 405.

CHAPTER VI

THE DEATH OF CHRIST

———————◄●►———————

THERE are two well-known pictures, each with the same title, "The Shadow of the Cross." One by Holman Hunt represents the interior of a carpenter's shop, with Joseph and the Boy Jesus at work. Mary also is present. The Boy Jesus pauses in His work, and as He stretches Himself the shadow of the Cross is formed on the wall. The other picture is a popular engraving which depicts the Infant Jesus running with outstretched arms to His mother, the shadow of the Cross being cast by His form as He runs. Both pictures are fanciful in form, but their underlying idea is assuredly true. If we read the Gospels just as they stand, it is clear that the death of Jesus Christ was really in view almost from the outset of His earthly appearance. At first sight there seems little in them about His death, but as we look deeper we see more. It was part of the Divine purpose and plan for Him from the first, and very early we have a hint of something like it in the words of the aged Simeon to the mother of our Lord: "A sword shall pierce through thine own soul also" (Luke ii. 35).

The impression that Jesus referred but little to His own death is due to a superficial reading of the Gospels. A closer acquaintance with them reveals the fact that at no period of His ministry was the thought of His death foreign to Him, and that during the last year of His life it was an ever-present and absorbing preoccupation.[1]

If, therefore, we would thoroughly understand the true idea of the life of Jesus Christ as it is recorded in the Gospels, it is essential for us to give special attention to what is said concerning His death. And our consideration must include two important inquiries: what the death meant as He Himself interpreted it, and what it meant as those nearest to Him interpreted it. Both these aspects are found quite clearly in the Gospels, while the latter is, of course, very definitely seen in the Acts and Epistles. No one can even glance at the New Testament without realising that for all its writers the death of Christ had a profound and far-reaching significance.

The revelation of the death was necessarily vague and fragmentary at first, but as time went on the fact and its purpose stood out in ever-increasing clearness. At the outset of His ministry (in Judæa) we find hints only, such as are implied in, "Destroy this Temple, and in three days I will raise it up" (John ii. 19); "The Son of Man must be lifted up" (John iii. 14). The same reserve is seen in the early days of the Galilean ministry in such a word as "The Bridegroom shall be snatched away" (Mark ii. 20, Greek). Another example of the same attitude is found in His reference to His death as a sign to His generation (Matt. xii. 40). On any interpretation of the allusion to Jonah the significance of the sign is admitted.[2] Later on, as the Galilean ministry was reach-

---

[1] Stalker, *The Christology of Jesus*, p. 173.
[2] *Contentio Veritatis*, p. 202.

ing its climax, came the discourses at Capernaum, when Christ spoke of His "flesh" which He would "give for the life of the world" (John vi. 51). These discourses provoked a crisis, and many of those who had professed allegiance left Him. From this point onwards retirement rather than publicity marked His ministry, and He gave Himself mainly to the work of training the Twelve. The dividing line between the general and specific teaching about His death is seen at Cæsarea Philippi. That which before had been implicit now becomes explicit. In the seclusion of that remote spot He asked His disciples what men were thinking of Him, and, in particular, what they themselves thought of Him. On eliciting from Peter the confession, "Thou art the Christ, the Son of the Living God," Jesus Christ clearly felt that the time had come when He could entrust them with further and fuller teaching concerning Himself. And so we read significantly, *"From that time forth* began Jesus to show unto His disciples, how that He must go unto Jerusalem, and suffer many things of the elders and chief priests and scribes, and be killed, and be raised again the third day" (Matt. xvi. 21). The emphasis on "From that time forth" (ἀπὸ τότε) compared with the similar phrase which marked the beginning of Christ's ministry (Matt. iv. 17) shows the importance of the new teaching. In this statement, together with two others uttered not long afterwards (Matt. xvii. 22 and xx. 18) Jesus Christ revealed certain circumstances of His death. It was to be contributed to by three causes—the Jewish authorities, His own disciples, and the Roman power. A careful study of these passages in the light of the previous silence about the death, so far as the first Gospel is concerned, clearly shows that in them we

have what has been rightly called the culminating idea
as to Himself and to His function.[1]

Later on the teaching becomes still more definite.
The purpose for which He is to die is stated. "The
Good Shepherd giveth His life for the sheep" (John x.
11). "The Son of Man came . . . to give His life a *ransom*
for many" (Matt. xx. 28). On the eve of the crucifixion,
other additions are made to the teaching about the purpose of His death. The corn of wheat must die if it is to
bear fruit (John xii. 24), and the greatest proof of love is
the laying down of life (John xv. 13). Then at the
institution of the Lord's Supper, Jesus Christ spoke of
His blood as that of the New Covenant shed for the
remission of sins (Matt. xxvi. 28).

Deeper and fuller still is the remarkable record of
Gethsemane and Calvary. As we read of the agony in
Gethsemane, we are impressed with the mystery of the
sufferings of Christ, and as we ponder His cry on the
Cross, we feel that we are in the presence of something
other than ordinary sufferings, and that His death was
indeed the "culminating idea" of His earthly ministry.

Not least of all, we cannot help observing the prominence of the story of the last week of our Lord's earthly
life in the record of the Gospels. Taking an ordinary
Bible, it is surprising to observe the space devoted to
the last week of the life and ministry of Christ, those
days which were spent in full expectation of and prepa-
ration for His imminent death. For example, out of
thirty pages devoted to the first Gospel, no less than ten
are given to the record of the last week. In the second
Gospel, out of nineteen pages seven are occupied with

---

[1] See Fairbairn, *The Philosophy of the Christian Religion*, ch. v.

the story from Palm Sunday to Easter Day. In St. Luke's Gospel no less than one-fourth is taken up with the story of these days, and out of twenty-four pages in the fourth Gospel ten are actually concerned with the same period. This prominence given to the events of the last few days demands attention and calls for explanation. In view of the crowded three years of Christ's ministry, is it not striking that there should be such fragmentariness in the story of those years until we come to the last few days? Surely the conspicuous place given to the death in the Gospels must mean that the writers regarded it as of supreme significance.

But there is something much more than this mere record of the Gospels concerning the death of Jesus Christ. When we review the entire situation we observe that two things stand out very prominently. The first is the utter inability of the disciples to understand this teaching about their Master's death. From the moment of the first disclosure, when Peter rebuked Jesus and repelled the idea of death with abhorrence (Matt. xvi. 22), they not only showed themselves unable to grasp its meaning, but for some time they would not even contemplate it as a fact. It was unwelcome and repellent to them, and they evidently did their utmost to shut their eyes to it. Later on, when further reference had been made and fuller details had been given, they were still apparently unable to grasp the fact. To us, as we read the story now, this persistent dulness is astonishing, though, in view of what was to happen, we may well regard it as "providential," for

It became a security to the Church for the truth of the Resurrection. The theory that they believed because they expected that He would rise again is against all evidence.[1]

[1] Plummer on St. Luke xviii. 34.

The response of James and John to the inquiry whether they could be baptised with His baptism and drink of His cup, is another illustration of this inability to enter into that which was already filling His soul, while the strife of the disciples as to who should be the greatest—a strife repeated on the very eve of the Crucifixion—is perhaps the most striking feature of the situation. This inability to understand and appreciate their Master's death, and the faithfulness with which this fact is recorded in the Gospels, constitute a very important feature of the problem of the death.

The other thing which stands out with equal prominence is the attitude of our Lord to His own death. Jesus Christ was truly man, and it is evident that He was deeply affected by the death which He so often mentioned and anticipated. It is not fanciful to see in the topic of the conversation on the Mount of Transfiguration some Divine encouragement to the Manhood of Christ: "Who . . . spake of His decease which He should accomplish at Jerusalem" (Luke ix. 31). One of the most remarkable and mysterious passages is found in connection with an announcement of His death to His disciples. "And they were in the way going up to Jerusalem; and Jesus went before them: and they were amazed: and as they followed they were afraid" (Mark x. 32). There was evidently something in His manner that impressed the disciples and gave rise to these feelings of awe and fear. Again, His reference to His "baptism" and His "cup" shows what was then in His mind as its overmastering thought and purpose. "The prospect of suffering was a perpetual Gethsemane." In the last week these feelings found their full expression on three separate occasions. The request of the Greeks to see Him was the occasion and apparently the cause of profound emotion. "Now is My soul troubled; and what shall I say? Father, save Me from this hour: but for this cause came I unto this hour" (John xii. 27). The Agony in Gethsemane is so sacred and mysterious that we shrink from discussing it, and yet we must observe that its record of sorrow, conflict, and submission is a revelation of Christ's consciousness which has a direct and important bearing on the meaning of the death. In a very real sense Calvary began in the Garden. And when we come to the last scene of all, the climax of the Cross, we are quite evidently in the atmosphere of something far exceeding, indeed quite different from, ordinary sufferings and death. The cry, "My God, My God, why hast Thou forsaken Me?" after all His wonderful life of fellowship, is the only time when the familiar term "Father" gave place to the more general one, "God." This must have had some deep meaning beyond anything ordinary and natural in connection with dying.

And so, as we think of the record of the death by itself in view of its place and prominence; as we think, moreover, of the effect of the announcement on the disciples; and, above all, as we ponder the effect of the anticipation of it on our Lord, we find ourselves face to face with a problem which must be taken into consideration and solved if we are to arrive at any full and adequate explanation of the manifestation of Jesus Christ on earth.

What, then, does the death of Jesus Christ mean? Why did He die? We know that He was in the prime of life; we know, too, that He ended His days after a time of immense popularity and widespread influence. What is the meaning of this catastrophe, so mysterious, so striking, so unmistakably predominant in the record of the Gospels?

Who spake of his decease which He should accomplish at Jerusalem.

It was not the death of a suicide, for did He not say, "I lay down My life of Myself"? The death was purely voluntary. *We* have to suffer: He need not have suffered. A word from Him might have saved His life. Nor was it an accidental death, for the obvious reason that it was foreseen, foretold, and prepared for in a variety of ways. Again, it was certainly not the death of a criminal, for no two witnesses could be found to agree together as to the charge against Him. Pilate declared that he found no fault in Him, and even Herod had not a word to say against Him. This, then, was no ordinary execution.

Some may say that the death of Jesus Christ was that of a martyr, and there is no doubt that as His death came at the hands of the Jews, and was a rejection of Him as their Messiah, there was in it an element of martyrdom for truth. But does this really explain the event? How are we to account for the unutterable sadness if Jesus Christ was a martyr? What, on this view, was the meaning of the mysterious agony in Gethsemane? When we recall the story of men like Stephen, Paul, and others who were martyred, and recall the triumphant joy and courage with which they met death, we are compelled to say either that Jesus Christ was inferior to them in the moment of death, or else that He was something more than a martyr.

Perhaps, however, we may think of His death as that of an example. This, no doubt, was part of the meaning, but it is obvious from the Gospels that it does not exhaust the idea. Death may come through a variety of circumstances, and some deaths are more painful than others. What, then, would be the value of the mere example of Jesus Christ in dying unless His death could in some way be an exact model for imitation for all who are called upon to die? Surely, therefore, we must search again before we can understand the true meaning of His death. Nor must we overlook the serious problem raised by Jesus Christ's death in connection with His personal character. The Jews charged Him with blasphemy because He made Himself the Son of God. If there was any misunderstanding in the meaning of this term, why did not Jesus correct it? It is clear that to the Jews this claim was tantamount to "making Himself equal with God" (John v. 18 and x. 33), and yet He suffered death for this without making any effort to show them their mistake. His character is therefore involved in the fact and meaning of His death.

The one and only adequate explanation of the death of Jesus Christ in the prime of life when He might have continued to exercise a powerful and marvellous influence over all the land of Palestine is that it was a sacrifice. And this is the account given to us in the Gospels. It was the death of One who was consciously innocent, of One whose life-work had been completed, of One who had come into this world for the very purpose of dying, of One whose death was foreseen, foretold, provided for. It is thus exceptional and unique, and this is clearly the impression of those who wrote the Gospels and the impression of every one who reads those Gospels honestly, fairly, and as a whole.

Its colour all through is the sacrificial colour, for Christ came not to be the mere Example, but also the Uplifter and the Redeemer of the world. We mark how as He drew near the close there were outbursts from a profound deep of sorrow. It was not that He had any secret remorse ravaging His heart. There had been no moment of madness in His holy years, no moment that He longed and prayed to pluck from out the past. There had been no moral tragedy, though He had His conflict with the enemy. No, His grief was not for Himself; it was for us. It was a burden of sympathy. He had come to deal not with our sorrows only, not with our darkness only—He had come to save us from our sins, and all the forces of His nature were strained that He might deliver us. And the load of our guilt, the chastisement of our peace, was upon Him all His years. Towards the end His burden-bearing is made more manifest. The secrets of His heart are more fully disclosed, but all the story is of one piece.[1]

Taking the Gospels, therefore, as we have received them, we are compelled to give attention to the remarkable and unique feature of the death of Jesus Christ under circumstances which might easily have been prevented if only He had been willing to do what His enemies wished Him to do. No one can mistake the profound impression made by that death on all the immediate disciples of Christ, and if we may be allowed for a moment to inquire how it impressed the early Church, and especially one of the greatest thinkers, the Apostle Paul, we find exactly the same effect. To that Apostle as to all the rest the death was the predominant fact and factor in the manifestation of Jesus Christ, and, as we know, St. Paul drew from it some of the deepest, profoundest, and most practical lessons for Christian people. No consideration of our present subject, therefore, can possibly overlook the fact and meaning of Christ's death as recorded in the New Testament. This fact, too, is unique among the religions of the world. The Founder of the religion dies, and that, as a sacrifice for sin. Whence came this idea? How are we to account for it? In view of the prominence, not to say predominance, of this feature in the rest of the New Testament,

[1] Robertson Nicoll, *The Church's One Foundation*, p. 46.

can we doubt that the source of the idea was Christ Himself? And if so, we are brought once again face to face with the consciousness of Christ as the great problem for solution.

CHAPTER VII

THE RESURRECTION OF CHRIST

———————◆●▶———————

THERE was one point on the battlefield of Waterloo which was taken and retaken three times during that memorable day. Both Napoleon and Wellington realised the strategical importance of the position and concentrated attention upon it. Its ultimate possession and retention by the British troops contributed largely to the final result. In the same way, there is one point in connection with Christianity which from the first has been felt to be vital and central—the Resurrection. As a consequence, the opponents of Christianity have always concentrated their attacks, and Christians have centred their defence upon it. Every one realises that it is vital, fundamental and essential. With this uncertain, everything else is uncertain; with this safe, all is safe. It is therefore of the utmost importance for our present inquiry that we should give attention to the subject of the Resurrection as it appears in the Gospels and as it is dealt with in the rest of the New Testament. There are several converging lines of evidence in support of the Resurrection, and not one of them can be overlooked. They include historical and moral proofs and each must have its place and weight. The issues at stake are so serious that nothing must be omitted. Christianity is either based on the fact of Christ or else it has no logical standing ground. What, then, are the lines of proof on which Christians base their belief in the Resurrection of Jesus Christ?

1. The first proof is the life and character of Jesus Christ Himself. It is always a keen disappointment when a life which commenced well finishes badly. We have this feeling even in fiction, an instinct which demands that a story should end well. Much more is this true of the life of Jesus Christ. A perfect life characterised by Divine claims ends in its prime in a cruel and shameful death. Is that an appropriate and fitting close? Are we satisfied? Surely there must be something else, for death could not end everything after such a noble career.

The Gospels give us the resurrection as the answer to these questions, and as the natural, inevitable issue of such a life. The Evangelists record the resurrection as the completion of the picture they draw of their Master. There is no real doubt that Christ anticipated and spoke of His own resurrection. At first He used only vague terms, such as, "Destroy this Temple, and in three days I will raise it up." But later on in His ministry He spoke quite plainly, and whenever he mentioned His death He added, "The Son of Man . . . must be raised the third day." These references to His resurrection are too numerous to be overlooked, and, in spite of all difficulties of detail, they are on any proper treatment of the Gospels an integral part of the claim made for Himself by Jesus Christ.[1] His veracity is therefore at stake if He

[1] Matt. xii. 38–40, xvi. 21, xvii. 23, xx. 19, xxvii. 63; Mark viii. 31, ix. 31, x. 34, xiv. 58; Luke ix. 22, xviii. 33; John ii. 19–21.

did not rise. Surely the word of such an One as Jesus Christ must be given due credence. We are therefore compelled to face the fact that the resurrection of which the Gospels speak is the resurrection of no ordinary man, but of *Jesus*—that is of one whose life and character had been unique, and for whose shameful death no proper explanation was possible or conceivable.

It is the resurrection of Jesus. If the witnesses had asserted about Herod, or about any ordinary person, what they did about Jesus, the presumption would have been all against them. The moral incongruity would have discredited their testimony from the first. But the resurrection was that of one in whom His friends had recognised while He lived, a power and goodness beyond the common measure of humanity, and they were sensible when it took place that it was in keeping with all they had known, hoped, and believed of Him.[1]

Consider, then, the resurrection in the light of what we have already advanced about the character of Christ. Is it possible that, in view of that perfect truthfulness of word and deed, there should be such a climax as is involved in a denial of His assurance that He would rise again?

If, then, it be admitted that the existence of the Gospel portrait of Christ is sufficient proof that it was drawn from life, and that He who is there portrayed laid claim to no knowledge affecting the outcome of His work which He did not possess, it must also be admitted that if He definitely stated that He would rise again from the dead, we have a strong *a priori* ground for believing that He did so rise.[2]

Consider, too, the death of Christ in the light of His perfect life. If that death was the close of a life so

---

[1] Denney, *Jesus and the Gospel*, p. 122 f.
[2] C. II. Robinson, *Studies in the Resurrection*, p. 30.

beautiful, so remarkable, so Godlike, we are faced with an insoluble mystery—the absolute and permanent triumph of wrong over right, and the impossibility of believing in truth or justice in the world.

It does not seem unreasonable to expect that God should vindicate in some striking and exceptional manner One who had trusted in Him completely, and who could truthfully say of Himself, "I do always those things that please Him."[1]

So the resurrection is not to be regarded as an isolated event, a fact in the history of Christ separated from all else. It must be taken in close connection with what precedes in the life of Him for whom resurrection is claimed. The true solution of the problem is to be found in that estimate of Christ which "most entirely fits in with the totality of the facts."[2]

2. Another line of proof is the fact of the empty grave and the disappearance of the body. That Jesus died and was buried, and that on the third morning the tomb was empty, cannot be seriously challenged. There have been those who have suggested the theory of a swoon and a recovery in the tomb, but to this, as Dr. Orr says, Strauss "practically gives its death-blow"[3] in words that may be usefully quoted again.

It is impossible that a being who had stolen half dead out of the sepulchre, who crept about weak and ill, wanting medical treatment, who required bandaging, strengthening, and indulgence, and who still at last yielded to His sufferings, could have given to His disciples the impression that He was a conqueror over death and the grave, the Prince of Life—an impression which lay at the bottom of their future ministry.[4]

---

[1] C. H. Robinson, *op. cit.*, p. 36.
[2] Orr, *The Resurrection of Jesus*, p. 14.
[3] Orr, *op. cit.*, p. 43.
[4] Quoted in C. H. Robinson, *Studies in the Resurrection of Christ*, p. 42.

At His burial a stone was rolled before the tomb, the tomb was sealed, and a guard was placed before it. Yet on the third morning the body had disappeared. There seem to be only two alternatives. His body must have been taken out of the grave by human hands or else by superhuman power. If the hands were human, they must have been those of His friends or of His foes. If His friends had wished to take out His body, the question at once arises whether they *could* have done so in the face of the stone, the seal, and the guard. If His foes had contemplated this action, the question arises whether they *would* have seriously considered the matter. Why should they do the very thing that would be most likely to spread the report of His resurrection? As Chrysostom said, "If the body had been stolen they could not have stolen it naked, because of the delay in stripping it of the burial cloths and the trouble caused by the drugs adhering to it."[1] There is therefore no other possibility but that the body was taken out of the tomb by superhuman power. How, too, is it possible to account for the failure of the Jews to disprove the Resurrection? We know that not more than seven weeks afterwards Peter preached in that very city the fact that Jesus had been raised. What would have been easier or more conclusive than for the Jews to have produced the dead body and silenced Peter for ever? As it has been truly said, "The silence of the Jews is as significant as the speech of the Christians."[2]

The fact of the empty tomb and the disappearance of the Body still remains a problem to be faced. By some writers the idea of resurrection is interpreted to mean

---

[1] Quoted in Day, *Evidence for the Resurrection*, p. 35.
[2] Fairbairn, *Studies in the Life of Christ*, p. 357.

the revival of Christ's spiritual influence on the disciples, which had been brought to a close by His death. It is thought that the essential idea and value of Christ's resurrection can be conserved, even while the belief in His bodily rising from the grave is surrendered.[1] But the various forms of the vision theory are now being gradually but surely regarded as inadequate and impossible. They are seen to involve the change of almost every fact in the Gospel history, and the invention of new scenes and conditions of which the Gospels know nothing.[2] From the physical standpoint, it has never been satisfactorily shown why the disciples should have had this abundant experience of visions, nor why they should have had it so soon after the death of Christ and within a strictly limited period, and why it suddenly ceased. And so in the present day the old theory of vision is virtually set aside, and for it is substituted the theory of a real spiritual manifestation of the risen Christ. The question at once arises whether this is not prompted by an unconscious but true desire to get rid of anything like a physical resurrection. Even though we may be ready to admit the reality of telepathic communication, it is impossible to argue that this is equivalent to the idea of resurrection. "The survival of the soul is not resurrection."[3] As some one once observed, "Whoever heard of a spirit being buried?"

In view of the records of the Gospels and the testimony of the New Testament generally, it is impossible to be "agnostic" as to what happened at the grave of Jesus, even though we are quite sure that He who died

[1] Orr, *The Resurrection of Jesus*, p. 23.
[2] Orr, *op. cit.*, p. 222.
[3] Orr, *op. cit.*, p. 229.

now lives and reigns. We are sometimes told that faith is not bound up with holding a particular view of the relations of Christ's present glory and the body that was once in Joseph's tomb, that faith is to be exercised in the exalted Lord, and that belief in a resuscitation of the human body is no vital part of it. It is no doubt perfectly true that our faith to-day is to be exercised solely in the exalted and glorified Lord, but surely faith must ultimately rest on fact, and it is difficult to understand how Christian faith can be really "agnostic" with regard to the facts about the empty tomb and the risen body, which are so prominent in the New Testament, and which form an essential part of the apostolic witness. The attempt to set faith and historical evidence in opposition to each other, which is so marked a characteristic of much modern thought, will never satisfy general Christian intelligence, and if there is to be any real belief in the historical character of the New Testament, it is impossible to be "agnostic" about facts that are writ so large on the face of the records.

And so we come again to that insuperable barrier, the empty tomb, which, together with the apostolic witness, stands impregnable against all the attacks of visional and apparitional theories. It is becoming more evident that these theories are entirely inadequate to account for the records in the Gospels, as well as for the place and power of those Gospels in the early Church and in all subsequent ages. The force of the evidence for the empty grave and the disappearance of the Body is clearly seen by the explanations suggested by various modern writers.[1] It will suffice to say that not one of

---

[1] Those of Oscar Holtzmann, K. Lake, and A. Meyer can be seen in Orr, *The Resurrection of Jesus*, ch. viii., and that of Reville in C. H. Robinson, *Studies in the Resurrection of Christ*, p. 69.

them is tenable without doing serious violence to the Gospel story, and also without putting forth new theories which are not only improbable in themselves, but are without a shred of real historical or literary evidence. The one outstanding fact which baffles all these writers is the empty grave.

Others suggest that resurrection means a real objective appearance of the risen Christ without implying any physical re-animation, that "the resurrection of Christ was an objective reality, but was not a physical resuscitation."[1] But the difficulty here is as to the meaning of the term "*re*surrection." If it means a *return* from the dead, a rising *again* (*re-*), must there not have been some identity between that which was put in the tomb and the "objective reality" which appeared to the disciples? No difficulty of conceiving of the resurrection of mankind hereafter must be allowed to set aside the plain facts of the record about Christ. It is, of course, quite clear that the resurrection Body of Jesus was not exactly the same as when it was put in the tomb, but it is equally clear that there was definite identity as well as definite dissimilarity, and both elements must be faced and accounted for. How the resurrection Body was sustained is a problem quite outside our ken, though the reference to "flesh and *bones*," compared with St. Paul's words about "flesh and *blood*" not being able to enter the Kingdom of God, may suggest that while the resurrection Body was not constituted upon a natural basis through blood, yet that it possessed "all things appertaining to the perfection of man's nature."[2] We may not be able to solve the problem, but we must hold fast to all the facts, and these

[1] C. H. Robinson, *op. cit.*, p. 12.
[2] Article IV.

may be summed up by saying that the Body was the same though different, different though the same. And so the true description of the resurrection seems to be that "it was an objective reality, but was not [merely] a physical resuscitation."

We are therefore brought back to a careful consideration of the facts recorded in the Gospels as to the empty tomb and the disappearance of the Body, and we only ask for an explanation which will take into consideration all the facts recorded, and will do no violence to any part of the evidence. To predicate a new resurrection Body in which Christ appeared to His disciples does not explain how in three days' time the Body which had been placed in the tomb was disposed of. Does not this theory demand a new miracle of its own?

There is much that must remain a mystery. We do not know how Christ was raised, nor with what manner of body He came. We cannot explain how that Body, which, as far as we know, had been subject in all respects to the laws to which all other bodies are subject, was so changed as to be able to pass out of time and space into infinity; but we do not know the origin and the essential nature even of that which is visible and tangible. And though we, who through the preaching of Christ's resurrection have reached a higher conception of eternal life than existed in the pre-Christian world, may be disposed to think that the resurrection of Christ would have been complete, even if His dead Body had turned to dust in the tomb where it was laid, it is difficult to see how in the first century the fact of Christ's perfect life after His death could have been made known to men apart from the resurrection of His body. Those who first appealed to the world to believe in the resurrection of Christ did so on the ground that they themselves had seen Him.[1]

---

[1] Kennett, *Interpreter*, vol. v. p. 271.

3. The next line of proof to be considered is the transformation of the disciples caused by the resurrection. They had seen their Master die, and through that death they lost all hope. Yet hope returned three days after. On the day of the crucifixion they were filled with sadness; on the first day of the week with gladness. At the crucifixion they were hopeless; on the first day of the week their hearts glowed with certainty and hope. When the message of the resurrection first came they were incredulous and hard to be convinced, but when once they became assured they never doubted again. What could account for the astonishing change in these men in so short a time? The mere removal of the Body from the grave could never have transformed their spirits and characters. Three days are not enough for a legend to spring up which would so affect them. Time is needed for a process of legendary growth. There is nothing more striking in the whole history of primitive Christianity than this marvellous change wrought in the disciples by a belief in the resurrection of their Master. It is a psychological fact that demands a full explanation.

4. From this fact of the transformation of personal life in so incredibly short a space of time, we proceed naturally to the next line of proof, the existence of the primitive Church.

There is no doubt that the Church of the Apostles believed in the Resurrection of their Lord.[1]

It is therefore true, and is now admitted on all hands, that the Church of Christ came into existence as the result of a belief in the resurrection of Christ. Leaving

---

[1] Burkitt, *The Gospel History and Its Transmission*, p. 74.

for further and fuller consideration the general question
of the Church's existence and progress, we are now
concerned only with its commencement as recorded in
the early chapters of the Book of the Acts of the Apostles, and there we see two simple and incontrovertible
facts: (1) The Christian society was gathered together
by preaching; (2) The substance of the preaching was
the resurrection of Jesus Christ. The Apostolic Church
is thus a result of a belief in the resurrection of Jesus
Christ. These early chapters of Acts bear the marks of
primitive documents, and their evidence is unmistakable. It is impossible to allege that the primitive Church
did not know its own history, that myths and legends
quickly grew up and were eagerly received, and that the
writers of the Gospels had no conscience for principle,
but manipulated their material at will. For as Dr. Orr
points out,[1] any modern Church could easily give an
account of its history for the past fifty years or more,
and it is simply absurd to think that the earliest Churches
had no such capability. In reality there was nothing
vague or intangible about the testimony borne by the
Apostles and other members of the Church. Archbishop
Alexander has well said, "As the Church is too holy for
a foundation of rottenness, so she is too real for a
foundation of mist."[2]

5. One man in the Apostolic Church must, however,
be singled out as a special witness for the resurrection.
The conversion of Saul of Tarsus is our next line of
proof. Leaving for fuller examination the testimony of
his whole life, we call attention to the evidence of his
writings to the resurrection of Jesus Christ. Some years

---

[1] Orr, *The Resurrection of Jesus*, p. 144.
[2] Alexander, *The Great Question*, p. 10.

ago an interesting article appeared in the *Expositor*[1] inquiring as to the conception of Christ which would be suggested to a heathen inquirer by a perusal of Paul's earliest extant writing (I Thessalonians). One point at least would stand out clearly—that Jesus Christ was killed (ch. ii. 15, iv. 14), and was raised from the dead (ch. iv. 14). As this Epistle is usually dated about A.D. 51—that is, only about twenty-two years after the resurrection—and as the same Epistle plainly attributes to Jesus Christ the functions of God in relation to men (ch. i. 1, i. 6, ii. 14, iii. 11), we can readily see the force of this testimony to the resurrection. Then a few years later, in an Epistle which is universally accepted as one of St. Paul's, we have a very much fuller reference to the resurrection. In the well-known chapter where he is concerned to prove (not Christ's resurrection, but) the resurrection of Christians, he naturally adduces Christ's resurrection as his greatest proof, and so gives a list of the various appearances of Christ after His resurrection, ending with one to himself, which he puts on an exact level with the others. "Last of all He was seen of me also." Now, quite apart from any consideration of the arguments based on the resurrection, we must give special attention to the nature and particularity of this testimony. "I delivered unto you first of all that which I also received, how that Christ died for our sins according to the Scriptures; and that He was buried, and that He rose again the third day according to the Scriptures." This, as it has been often pointed out, is our earliest authority for the appearances of Christ after the resurrection, and dates from within thirty years of the event itself. But there is much more than this. As Professor Kennett says—

[1] E. Medley, Fifth Series, vol. iv. p. 359.

Important as this consideration is, it is of even greater importance to notice that St. Paul expressly claims that the account of the death, burial, and resurrection of Christ, which he states with the precision of a formal creed, is not something which has only recently taken shape, when men's memories have begun to fail, but something which he himself learned in substantially the same form when he first became a Christian. In other words, he affirms that within five years of the crucifixion of Jesus he was taught that "Christ died for our sins according to the Scriptures; and that He was buried, and that He rose again the third day according to the Scriptures."[1]

And if we seek to appreciate the full bearing of this act and testimony we have a right to draw the same conclusion as Professor Kennett and

Maintain that within a very few years of the time of the crucifixion of Jesus, the evidence for the resurrection of Jesus was, in the mind of at least one man of education, absolutely irrefutable.[2]

Besides, we find this narrative of St. Paul includes one small but significant statement which at once recalls a very definite feature of the Gospel tradition—the mention of "the third day." A reference to the passages in the Gospels where Jesus Christ spoke of His resurrection will show how prominent and persistent was this note of time. Why, then, should Paul have introduced it in his statement? Was it part of the teaching which he had "received"? What is the significance of this plain emphasis on the *date* of the resurrection? Is it not this, that it bears absolute testimony to the empty tomb? Professor Kennett well sums up the argument on this point, and with it the testimony of St. Paul—

[1] *Interpreter*, vol. v. p. 267.
[2] Ibid.

It may be claimed, then, for the story of the empty tomb, that St. Paul heard it, and, what is more, *believed* it, in Jerusalem at a date when the recollection of the tomb was fresh in people's minds; when it would have been possible for him to examine it and see for himself whether it was empty or not, and, if it were empty, to make full inquiries when and by whom it was discovered that it no longer contained the body of Jesus; at a date, moreover, when the hostility to the new doctrine must have exposed its adherents to the fiercest cross-questioning as to the reasons for their belief, especially when, as in the case of St. Paul, they had been identified with the anti-Christian party. Saul of Tarsus, the promising pupil of Gamaliel, who seemed the coming man in Judaism, threw away all his prospects for the belief in Christ's resurrection, turned his friends into foes, and exchanged a life of honourable ease for a life of toil and shame— surely common sense requires us to believe that that for which he so suffered was in his eyes established beyond the possibility of doubt.[1]

In view, therefore, of St. Paul's personal testimony to his own conversion, his interviews with those who had seen Jesus Christ on earth before and after His resurrection, and not least the prominence given to the resurrection in the Apostle's own teaching, we may fairly challenge afresh the attention of to-day to the evidence of St. Paul for the resurrection. It is a well-known story how that Lord Lyttelton and his friend Gilbert West left the University at the close of one academic year each determining to give attention respectively during the long vacation to the conversion of St. Paul and the resurrection of Christ, in order to prove the baselessness of both. They met again in the autumn and compared

[1] *Interpreter*, vol. v. p. 271.

experiences. Lord Lyttelton had become convinced of
the truth of St. Paul's conversion, and Gilbert West of
the resurrection of Jesus Christ. If, therefore, Paul's
twenty-five years of suffering and service for Christ was
a reality, his conversion was true, for everything he did
began with that sudden change. And if his conversion
was true, Jesus Christ rose from the dead, for everything Paul was and did he attributed to the sight of the
risen Christ.

6. The next line of proof of the resurrection is the
record in the Gospels of the appearances of the risen
Christ, and it is the *last* in order to be considered. By
some writers it is put first, but this is in forgetfulness of
the dates when the Gospels were written. It is obvious
on a moment's thought that the resurrection was believed in by the Christian Church for a number of years
before our Gospels were written, and that it is therefore
impossible for the record of the Gospels to be our
primary and most important evidence. We must get
behind the Gospels if we are to appreciate to the full the
force and variety of the evidence for the resurrection. It
is for this reason that, following the proper logical order,
we have reserved to the last our consideration of the
appearances of the risen Christ as given in the Gospels.
The point is one of great importance.

So far as the fact of the resurrection of Jesus is concerned,
the narratives of the Evangelists are quite the least important
part of the evidence with which we have to deal. It is no
exaggeration to say that if we do not accept the resurrection
on grounds which lie outside this area, we shall not accept it
on the grounds presented here. The real historical evidence
for the resurrection is the fact that it was believed, preached,
propagated and produced its fruit and effect in the new

phenomenon of the Christian Church, long before any of our Gospels was written. This is not said to disparage the Gospels, or to depreciate what they tell, but only to put the question on its true basis. Faith in the resurrection was not only prevalent, but immensely powerful before any of our New Testament books were written.[1]

Now, with this made clear, we proceed to consider the evidence afforded by the records of the post-resurrection appearances of Christ. Modern criticism of the Gospels during recent years has tended to adopt the view that Mark is the earliest, and Matthew and Luke are dependent on it. This view is said to be "the one solid result"[2] of the literary criticism of the Gospels. If this is so, the question of the records of the resurrection becomes involved in the difficult problem about the supposed lost ending of St. Mark, which, according to modern criticism, would thus close without any record of an appearance of the risen Christ. On this, however, two things may be said at the present juncture. (1) There are some indications that the entire question of the criticism of the Gospels is to be re-opened.[3] (2) Even if the current theory be accepted, it would not seriously weaken the intrinsic force of the evidence for the resurrection, because, after all, Mark does not invent or "doctor" his material, but embodies the common apostolic tradition of his time.[4] We may therefore meanwhile examine the record of the appearances without finding them essentially affected by any particular theory of the origin and relations of the Gospels.

[1] Denney, *Jesus and the Gospel*, p. 111.
[2] W. C. Allen, "St. Matthew," *International Critical Commentary*, Preface, p. vii.; Burkitt, *The Gospel History*, p. 37.
[3] Ramsay, *St. Luke the Physician*, ch. ii. See also Orr, *The Resurrection of Jesus*, p. 63 ff.
[4] Orr, *op. cit.*, p. 62.

There are two sets of appearances, one in Jerusalem and the other in Galilee, and their number and the amplitude and weight of their testimony should be carefully estimated. While we are precluded by our space from examining each appearance minutely, and indeed it is unnecessary for our purpose to do so, it is impossible to avoid calling attention to two of them. No one can read the story of the walk to Emmaus (Luke xxiv.), or of the visit of Peter and John to the tomb (John xx.), without observing the clear and striking marks of reality and personal testimony in the accounts.[1] The Bishop of Durham calls attention to these in discussing the former incident.

It carries with it, as great literary critics have pointed out, the deepest inward evidences of its own literal truthfulness. For it so narrates the intercourse of "a risen God" with commonplace men as to set natural and supernatural side by side in perfect harmony. And to do this has always been the difficulty, the despair of imagination. The alternative has been put reasonably thus: St. Luke was either a greater poet, a more creative genius, than Shakespeare, or—he did not create the record. He had an advantage over Shakespeare. The ghost of Hamlet was an effort of laborious imagination. The risen Christ on the road was a fact supreme, and the Evangelist did but tell it as it was.[2]

Other writers whose attitude to the Gospel records is very different from that of the Bishop of Durham bear the same testimony to the impression of truth and reality made upon them by the Emmaus narrative.[3]

It is well known that there are difficulties connected with the number and order of these appearances, but they are probably due largely to the summary character

[1] Latham, *The Risen Master*, ch. i.
[2] Moule, *Meditations for the Church's Year*, p. 108.
[3] A. Meyer and K. Lake. Quoted in Orr, *op. cit.*, p. 176 f.

of the story, and are not sufficient to invalidate the uniform testimony to two facts: (1) the empty grave, (2) the appearances of Christ on the third day. These are the main facts of the combined witness. [1] The very difficulties which have been observed in the Gospels for nearly nineteen centuries are a testimony to a conviction of the truth of the narratives on the part of the whole Christian Church. The Church has not been afraid to leave these records as they are because of the facts that they embody and express. If there had been no difficulties men might have said that everything had been artificially arranged, whereas the differences bear testimony to the reality of the event recorded. The very fact that we possess these two sets of appearances—one in Jerusalem and one in Galilee—is really an argument in favour of their credibility, for if it had been recorded that Christ had appeared in Galilee only or Jerusalem only, it is not unlikely that the account might have been rejected for lack of support. It is well known that records of eye-witnesses often vary in details while there is no question as to the events themselves. The various books recording the story of the Indian Mutiny, or the surrender of Napoleon at Sedan, are cases in point, and Sir William Ramsay has shown the entire compatibility of certainty as to the main fact with great uncertainty as to precise details. [2] We believe, therefore, that a careful examination of these appearances will afford evidence of a chain of circumstances extending from the empty grave to the day of the ascension.

When we examine carefully all these converging lines of evidence and endeavour to give weight to all the facts of the case, it seems impossible to escape from the

[1] Orr, *The Resurrection of Jesus*, p. 212.
[2] Ramsay, *St. Paul the Traveller*, p. 29.

problem of a physical miracle. That the *primâ facie* view of the evidence afforded by the New Testament suggests a miracle, and that the Apostles really believed in a true physical resurrection, are surely beyond all question. And yet very much of present-day thought refuses to accept the miraculous. The scientific doctrine of the uniformity and continuity of nature bars the way, so that from the outset it is concluded that miracles are impossible. We are either not allowed to believe,[1] or else we are told that we are not required to believe,[2] in the re-animation of a dead body. If we take this view, "there is no need, really, for investigation of evidence; the question is decided before the evidence is looked at."[3]

We venture to question and even to challenge the tenableness of this position. It proves too much. If we are not allowed to believe in any Divine intervention which we may call supernatural or miraculous, it is difficult to see how we are to account for the Person of Christ at all. "A Sinless Personality would be a miracle in time." If it be said that no amount of evidence can establish a fact which is miraculous, we have still to account for the moral miracles which are really involved in and associated with the resurrection, especially the deception of the disciples, who could have found out the truth of the case; a deception, too, that has proved so great a blessing to the world. And if we are not to believe in the possibility of physical resuscitation, then obviously the miracles recorded as wrought by Christ on Jairus's daughter, the young man of Nain, and Lazarus at once go by the board. Surely to those who hold a

---

[1] See Orr, *op. cit.*, p. 44.
[2] C.II. Robinson, *Studies in the Resurrection of Christ*, ch. ii.
[3] Orr, *op. cit.*, p. 46.

true theistic view of the world this *a priori* view is impossible. Are we to refuse to allow to God at least as much liberty as we possess ourselves? Is it really thinkable that God has less spontaneity of action than ourselves? *We* may like or dislike, give or withhold, will or not will, but the course of nature must flow on unbrokenly. Surely God cannot be conceived of as having given such a constitution to the universe as limits in the least His power to intervene if necessary and for sufficient purpose with the work of His own hands. Not only are all things *of* Him, but all things are *through* Him and *to* Him. The resurrection means the presence of miracle, and "there is no evading the issue with which this confronts us."[1] Unless, therefore, we are prepared to accept the possibility of the miraculous, all explanation of the New Testament evidence is a pure waste of time.

And so we come back to a consideration of the various lines of proof. Taking them singly, they must be admitted to be strong, but taking them altogether, the argument is cumulative and sufficient, if it is not overwhelming. Thomas Arnold of Rugby, no mean judge of historical evidence, said that the resurrection was the best attested fact in human history. Christianity welcomes all possible sifting, testing, and use by those who honestly desire to arrive at the truth, and if they will give proper attention to all the facts and factors involved, we believe they will come to the conclusion expressed years ago by the Archbishop of Armagh, that the resurrection is the rock from which all the hammers of criticism have never chipped a single fragment.[2]

---

[1] Orr, *The Resurrection of Jesus*, p. 53.
[2] *The Great Question*, p. 24.

CHAPTER VIII

THE GOSPELS OF CHRIST

WE have now endeavoured to consider the picture of
Jesus Christ as it is presented to us in the Gospels—His
character, claim, teaching, death, and resurrection. It is
necessary, however, at this stage to consider one feature
which is apt to be overlooked. Indeed its very familiar-
ity tends to make us forget its force and importance. It
is this: taking the Gospels as they stand, how are we to
account for the delineation of Jesus Christ as there
given? What is the relation between the character of
Christ and the record in which it is found? The alternatives are only two: either the character is real, or else it
was created by the writers. The value of this argument
is such that it can be thoroughly examined and tested
by even the most untrained mind, and it requires no
technical scholarship and no presupposition of the Divine authority or inspiration of the Gospels. This is
therefore a point of real importance because of its simplicity and directness, and the universality of its application.

It is the character of Jesus Christ which furnishes the most
powerful argument for the historical character of the records

in which it is portrayed. The examination of historical records is the work of trained experts, and at the end of the
examination nothing more than a high degree of probability
can be attained. The examination of the consistency of a
certain character, however, is a much simpler matter, and
yields an absolute certainty. The character of Jesus Christ
stands or falls according as the drawing of it in the Gospel
narratives is consistent or inconsistent. Its absolute consistency
guarantees its reality.[1]

Let us then state the argument again; either the character of Jesus Christ is real or else it was created by the
writers. The character, as we observe it in the Gospels,
bears every mark of reality, every indication of living
personality.

It is almost a law of literature that any portraits of the ideal
in the least degree satisfactory are closely transcribed from
life, as was, for example, Dinah Morris in *Adam Bede*. This
confirms what has been said. The wonderfulness, the originality of the character described in the Gospels, the minuteness,
the freshness, the realisation, the detail of the whole portrait,
prove that it is drawn from life.[2]

Now we know who and what were the writers; they
were ordinary men without any pretence to literary
ability, still less to literary genius. And yet they have
managed to depict for us a unique Figure which has
been the greatest attraction of the ages. How are we to
account for this even on purely literary grounds? Can
we imagine such men inventing such a character? Is not
the conception beyond anything merely human? As Dr.
Fairbairn has well said—

Were the Gospels inventions, whether mythical or con-

---

[1] B. Lucas, *The Faith of a Christian*, p. 46.
[2] Robertson Nicoll, *The Church's One Foundation*, p. 43.

scious, spontaneous or purposed, they would be the most marvellous creations of literary art which we possess.[1]

Have we anything in literature at all like it? If we take the finest characters of history or the noblest ideal in fiction, we at once see the contrast. In all the world's great masterpieces we cannot find a single instance of a perfect human character. We think of Hamlet as perhaps the most perfect delineation of human character in Shakespeare's works, but no one would dream of saying that he was anything like a perfect human being. To paint the ideal is much, even for genius, but to picture the sinless is very much more. And yet in these Gospels, written by men possessing no literary genius, we have a perfect Human Being depicted.

They succeeded in giving us the Figure of the Sinless. The pencil does not swerve; and yet how inevitable it was that it should swerve had another Hand not held it! One false note would have destroyed all, but that false note never comes.[2]

And, what is in its way more remarkable than anything else, the sum total of the impression made by this sinless and perfect Being is one of absolute naturalness, with the entire absence of anything incongruous, unbalanced, or unfitting.

The remarkable thing is not simply that these attributes and acts are represented as His, but that they are conceived as quite natural to Him, as not making Him anomalous or abnormal, but as leaving Him simple and rational and real—a person who never ceases to be Himself, who has no double consciousness and plays no double part, but expresses Himself in history according to the nature He has and the truth within Him. There is nothing quite like this in literature, no

[1] Fairbairn, *The Philosophy of the Christian Religion*, p. 303.
[2] Robertson Nicoll, *op. cit.*, p. 47.

miraculous person who is so truly natural, so continuously one and the same; and no writers of the miraculous who so feel that they are dealing with what is normal and regular through and through. These are things which have more than a psychological interest; they speak of men who have stood face to face with the reality, and are conscious of only describing what they saw.[1]

How is all this to be explained? Did the Person create the record, or did the record create the Person? If the writers of the Gospels can be conceived of as inventing the character of Jesus Christ, it is hardly too much to say that we should be face to face with at least as great a miracle as anything we now possess in connection with Christianity. This has been admitted by several leading opponents of Christianity. Thus, Theodore Parker—

It takes a Newton to forge a Newton. What man could have fabricated a Jesus? No one but a Jesus.[2]

And John Stuart Mill in like manner—

It is of no use to say that Christ, as exhibited in the Gospels, is not historical, and that we know not how much of what is admirable has been superadded by the tradition of His followers. Who among His disciples or among their proselytes was capable of inventing the sayings of Jesus, or of imagining the life and character revealed in the Gospels? Certainly not the fishermen of Galilee; as certainly not St. Paul, whose character and idiosyncrasies were of a totally different sort; still less the early Christian writers, in whom nothing is more evident than that all the good in them was derived, as they always professed it was derived, from the higher source.[3]

Rousseau's words, too, are often quoted—

---

[1] Fairbairn, *The Philosophy of the Christian Religion*, p. 330.
[2] Theodore Parker, *Life of Jesus*, p. 363.
[3] Mill, *Essays on Nature*, pp. 253–255.

It is more inconceivable that several men should have united to forge the Gospel than that a single person should have furnished the subject of it. The gospel has marks of truth so great, so striking, so perfectly inimitable, that the inventor of it would be more astonishing than the hero.[1]

To believe that unlettered Galilean fishermen, or even their immediate successors, invented a character which is so transcendent as to cast into the shade the finest efforts of all the greatest writers of every age, requires greater credulity than to believe that such a life was actually lived. And besides this, the individuality of each of the writers, so marked that an ordinary reader sometimes thinks one contradicts another, joined with the marvellous unity of the picture, which is clear to the mind of every student together with the absence of all sophistry or special pleading, will not allow us to believe that the facts given are anything else than an accurate record by honest men of what they saw and heard. If Jesus was acclaimed, they put it down; if He was scorned, they recorded it. When He was called liar, blasphemer, deceiver, devil, when His own townsmen rejected His claims, they drew no veil over the unpalatable circumstances, but let the truth be put down just as it was. Where else can we find the biographer of whom these things may be said?

It is inconceivable that the Evangelic Jesus should be a creation, whether of some master mind or of the myth-forming genius of the primitive Church. Humanity cannot transcend itself. Surely scepticism has its credulity no less than faith when it is gravely maintained that so radiant an ideal arose "among nearly the most degraded generation of the most narrow-minded race that the world has ever known, and made it the birthplace of a new earth." The mere fact

[1] See Robertson Nicoll, *The Church's One Foundation*, p. 41.

that there dawned on the world, and that in a land barren of wisdom and an age morally bankrupt, an ideal which has been the wonder and inspiration of mankind for more than sixty generations, is an irrefragable evidence that is no mere ideal, but a historic fact. The Divine Life which the Evangelists portray must have been actually lived out on the earth, else they could never have conceived it. And thus the Evangelic Jesus is Himself the supreme evidence at once of the historicity of the evangelic narratives and of His own Divinity.[1]

It will readily be seen from what has been said that this argument is quite independent of any theory we may hold as to the origin, dates, and primitive character of the Gospels. It is the picture itself that has to be accounted for. There is no reasonable doubt that our four Gospels have occupied their present place in the Church at least since A.D. 200, whatever may have been their history previous to that date. How, then, are we to explain the picture of Christ? And even when we go further and accept the irreducible minimum of the Gospels allowed us by modern criticism, the general result is exactly the same.[2] Analyse the Gospels as we will, the Portrait is there. Not only so, but the more complex the origin and the more numerous the strata of the Gospels, the greater the problem of the Portrait. Even if we admit the presence of inaccuracies, inconsistencies, later additions, and interpolations, the Character remains and has to be accounted for. The larger the number of authorities, the more difficult to account for the unity. How is it that the net result of so many different hands at so many different times should be the perfect Picture,

---

[1] *Religion and the Modern Mind.* David Smith, "The Divinity of Jesus," p. 176.

[2] Nolloth, *The Person of our Lord and Recent Thought*, chapters iii. and iv.

the consistent, balanced delineation of Jesus Christ as it stands in the Gospels to-day? And how and why, too, did this happen just then in Judæa, under such adverse conditions? Why was the Perfect Man depicted then, and not before or since? How is it that the Gospels remain unique in literature to-day? Among the striking proofs of this uniqueness is the contrast afforded by the apocryphal Gospels.

All who read them with any attention will see that they are fictions, and not histories; not traditions even, so much as legends . . . Before I undertook this work I never realised so completely as I do now the impassable character of the gulf which separates the genuine Gospels from these.[1]

Again: we may look at the question from the standpoint of modern criticism of the Gospels which, as we have already seen, regards Mark, or a document equivalent to our Mark, as the earliest Gospel. Does the acceptance of this position make any difference to the conception of Christ formed by readers? None whatever. The earliest Gospel is as full of the picture of a perfect and supernatural Christ as the later ones. This is admitted by critics who do not accept the orthodox Christian view of Christ and Christianity. Let us quote some representative testimonies of well-known scholars—

Even the oldest Gospel is written from the standpoint of faith; already for Mark Jesus is not only the Messiah of the Jewish people, but the miraculous, eternal Son of God, whose glory shone in the world.[2]
For the belief of the community, which is shared already by the oldest Evangelist, Jesus is the miraculous Son of God,

---

[1] B. Harris Cowper, Preface to Translation of the *Apocryphal Gospels*.
[2] Quoted, Warfield, *The Lord of Glory*, p. 144, from Bousset, *Was Wissen Wir von Jesus?*

on whom men believe, whom men put wholly by God's side.[1]

Nor must we lose sight of the fact that the Gospels, whenever and by whomsoever written, represent not merely four men, the writers, but the entire Christian community among whom they arose and by whom they were universally accepted. The picture of Christ of the earliest Gospel is the Christ of the Christian Church, not only of the Evangelists. To quote Bousset again—

We have not merely pupils transmitting the teaching of their Master, but a believing community speaking of one they honour as the exalted Lord.[2]

So also Otto Schmiedel—

The early Church, in whose circles the narratives of the life of Jesus originated . . . was at one in its acknowledgement of Christ, its exalted Lord.[3]

As, therefore, we study closely the most recent and acutest criticism of the Gospels in the light of the generally accepted view that Mark is the earliest, it is impossible to doubt or question the conclusion drawn by Professor Warfield—

It is clear, then, that the documents which, even in the view of the most unreasonable criticism, are supposed to underlie the structure of our present Synoptics, are freighted with the same teaching which these Gospels themselves embody as to the Person of our Lord. Literary criticism cannot penetrate to any stratum of belief more primitive than this. We may sink our trial shafts down through the soil of the Gospel tradition at any point we please; it is only conform-

---

[1] Quoted, Warfield, *The Lord of Glory.*

[2] Quoted, Warfield, *op. cit.*, p. 144, from Bousset, *Was Wissen Wir von Jesus?*

[3] Quoted, Warfield, *op. cit.*, p. 133, from O. Schmiedel, *Die Hauptprobleme der Leben-Jesu Forschung.*

able strata that we pierce. So far as the tradition goes, it gives consentient testimony to an aboriginal faith in the Deity of the Founder of the religion of Christianity.[1]

It will be seen that our argument in this chapter has proceeded on two distinct though connected lines. The one is that of taking the Gospels as they stand, and as they have stood since A.D. 200, and seeking to account for their picture of Jesus Christ. The other is that of accepting the consensus of modern criticism as to our earliest Gospel and endeavouring to account for the picture and view of Christ there given. In both cases the result is the same; a supernatural Person is depicted and has to be accounted for. And this is surely sufficient, whatever criticism may say as to the origin and date of our Gospels.

When Christians are asked to furnish a reply to every fresh assault on the Gospel history, they are entitled to say that if they can establish the great faiths of the historic creed, the critic who denies these, and justifies the denial on the grounds of criticism, must be in error. To establish the sinlessness of Christ and His Resurrection is virtually to refute many critical arguments.[2]

But, as a matter of fact, the best of modern scholarship tends more and more to put back our Gospels to the position of contemporary documents, and to see in them the testimony of eye-witnesses to the Person and circumstances there recorded.

The more these works are studied the more conviction will grow that they were written by men who had companied with eye-witnesses of the Saviour's life and who have faithfully reported their words.[3]

---

[1] Warfield, *op. cit.*, p. 141. See also pp. 157, 158.
[2] Robertson Nicoll, *The Church's One Foundation*, p. 11
[3] Salmon, *Introduction to the New Testament*, p. 581.

That the third Gospel and the Acts are by Luke, a companion of Paul, is now fully admitted by Harnack. The momentous consequence of this as a testimony to early date and contemporary knowledge is perfectly obvious to all who have given attention to the subject[1]

And even with the inclusion of the fourth Gospel this position is scarcely weakened. Dr. Sanday, speaking of St. John xxi. 24, says—

This is the most explicit of all the passages which imply that the author of the Gospel was an eye-witness, and wrote as an eye-witness. . . . There is no ambiguity in the verse . . . A statement like this if not true is deliberately false; and if it is false, then I should say that the writer stamped himself as dishonest and insincere.[2]

In the same way the Dean of Westminster says—

It is to my mind impossible to doubt that the Evangelist of the fourth Gospel intended the scenes which he described to be accepted as real occurrences; it is impossible to believe that he knew them all the while to be the outcome of his imagination.[3]

The more thoroughly the Gospels are studied the stronger will be the conviction that they have come from men who were eye-witnesses of Christ and who have faithfully reported the events of their Master's life. Dr. Kenyon, of the British Museum, closes a valuable essay by referring to the evidence which has become available during recent years for the study of the Gospels.

[1] Harnack, *Luke the Physician*, passim. See also Ramsay, *Luke The Physician*, ch. i.

[2] Sanday, *Expository Times*, vol. xx. p. 154.

[3] Armitage Robinson, *The Historical Character of St. John's Gospel*, p. 9.

So far as they have borne upon the question at all, the tendency has been the same—to confirm the traditional view of the date and authority of our Gospels. The traditional view had been hotly assailed by the searching historical criticism which, for good or for evil (and certainly very largely for good) has beaten upon the Christian records during the last sixty years, as it has upon all other departments of human knowledge; and although the great defenders of that tradition made good their case with the materials which already lay to their hands, it is a striking fact that witness after witness has risen, as it were, from the grave to testify that they were right. The historical critic will accept the new evidence and record it, after the searching examination which it requires, with that loyal obedience to the established fact which is characteristic of the best criticism of the day; but the Christian student is entitled to go one step further, and to say: "This is the Lord's doing, and it is marvellous in our eyes."[1]

And so from the Gospels themselves, their conception of Christ, their reality and candour,[2] we argue for our position that Christ is Christianity. We invite the closest scrutiny, and ask men to submit the Gospels to the severest tests, feeling confident of the conclusion when all the facts and factors are properly taken into account.

We are confronted by the story of the Gospels. However critically we may analyse them, the marvellous picture which they have created remains. And it is that picture, and not any critical explanations of it, which has dominated human history for nigh upon two thousand years. And what is that picture? It professes, in the form in which it has come down to us, to be a revelation of God to man. It has the very characteristics which we might imagine such a revelation to possess; for it startles, it surprises us, it takes away our

[1] Kenyon, *the Gospels in the Early Church*, p. 48, "Essays of the Times," No. 3.

[2] See a suggestive article in the *Spectator* for Jan. 30, 1909, on "The Candour of the new Testament."

breath; it is utterly unlike what we should have expected; we could never have invented it. And yet the longer we look at it, the more truly Godlike it appears. It is not what we thought God would be like, if we could see Him, but it surpasses our utmost thought. It is too superhuman not to be true. And not only so, but it has subserved the purpose, the only purpose, for which a revelation could be made. It has drawn all its serious believers into the experience of a closer communion with God. It has introduced in consequence a new type of spiritual life into the world. It has ennobled the whole subsequent history of our race. Can it be other than the revelation which, as Theists, we must antecedently expect?[1]

This, then, is the problem of the Gospels in relation to Christ, and we are not surprised that men of very different schools of thought have realised its force and admitted its power. Thus Professor Gwatkin says—

There is a tremendous dilemma there which will have to be faced. Assuming that the stupendous claim ascribed to him is false, one would think it must have disordered his life with insanity if he made it himself, and the accounts of his life if others invented it.[2]

And a very different thinker, Matthew Arnold, whose attitude to orthodox Christianity is well known, writes—

Jesus himself as He appears in the Gospels, and for the very reason that He is so manifestly above the heads of His reporters there, is, in the jargon of modern philosophy, an *absolute*; we cannot explain Him, and cannot get behind Him and above Him, cannot command Him.[3]

Is there any solution of this problem except that which the New Testament and the Christian Church provide?

[1] Illingworth, *Reason and Revelation*, p. 151.
[2] Gwatkin, *The Knowledge of God*, vol. i. p. 120.
[3] Matthew Arnold, Preface to *Literature and Dogma*.

CHAPTER IX

THE CHURCH OF CHRIST

————— ◄•► —————

WHEN we stand on the Nore Lightship we see the Thames at its mouth; when we stand on the Cotswold Hills at Thames-head we see the great river at its source. When we look over the world to-day we see Christianity as a great and almost world-wide fact; but the stream must have had a source, the effect must have had a cause. Here all around us is the community which men call the Christian Church, the various communities which make up the totality of Christian profession. How did they come into being originally? For our present purpose we take the Church in its widest sense, "the blessed company of all faithful people," or "all who profess and call themselves Christians."

How did the Church begin? It has been well said that "the Church of Christ is built on an empty grave." Seven weeks after the Crucifixion the Apostle Peter preached in Jerusalem the resurrection of Jesus Christ; the weak and cowardly disciple was transformed into the bold witness, and in language as plain as it could possibly be, he declared to the Jews their sin of crucifying Christ, and the work of God in raising Him from the dead. Not only was there no attempt on the part of the Jews to deny the Apostle's words, but, on the contrary, no less than three thousand of them believed what he said, accepted his word, obeyed his exhortation, and became united together in a new fellowship through his teaching and the ordinances of Baptism and the Holy Communion. There is no possibility of doubting that these men were drawn together into this new community by their separate individual new relation to Christ. Thus and thus only the Church began.

How did the Church continue? By the proclamation of the same message on the part of the Apostolic preachers, and by the reception of that message on the part of their hearers. Wherever they went the substance of their teaching was "Jesus and the Resurrection," and wherever it was given it was received through faith, and faith expressed itself in the ordinances of Baptism and the Holy Communion as proofs of relationship to God, and also as marks of fellowship between those who professed and called themselves Christians. This apostolic testimony meant persecution, ostracism, and not seldom death. Why should they have thus been willing to suffer? Why did they not remain silent, go to their homes in Galilee and prevent the Jewish authorities from hearing of them from that time forward? The answer is that they could not but speak of the things which they had seen and heard. Jesus Christ was a reality to them, and out of a full heart they preached Him as a living Saviour and Lord. This is the fact that stands out prominently from the Day of Pentecost onwards through the entire New Testament—the fact of a new community whose one tie of fellowship was their relation to Christ, their common Master.

When we open the New Testament we find ourselves in presence of a glowing religious life. There is nothing in the world which offers any real parallel either to this life or to the collection of books which attests it. The soul, which in contemporary literature is bound in shallows and in miseries, is here raised as on a great tidal wave of spiritual blessing. Nothing that belongs to a complete religious life is wanting, neither convictions nor motives, neither penitence nor ideals, neither vocation nor the assurance of victory. And from beginning to end, in all its parts and aspects and elements, this religious life is determined by Christ. It owes its character at every point to Him.[1]

Even a cursory study of the New Testament reveals the fact that the one and only thing that united men of different races, creeds, temperaments, and grades was their relation to Christ, while

The most careful scrutiny of the New Testament discloses no trace of a Christianity in which Jesus has any other place than that which is assigned Him in the faith of the historical Church.[2]

And the same thing is true of the books of the New Testament as records of teaching. In spite of the great and striking differences of aspect, standpoint, and substance between such writers as Paul, John, James, Peter, and Luke, there is nothing more striking than the essential unity amid all these remarkable differences. This unity is simply that of a common attitude to Jesus Christ. Whatever they have to record or teach converges towards Him, and has Him for its theme and object.

There is a unity in all these early Christian books which is powerful enough to absorb and subdue their differences, and

[1] Denney, *Jesus and the Gospel*, p. 1.
[2] Denney, *op. cit.*, p. 373.

that unity is to be found in a common religious relation to Christ, a common debt to Him, a common sense that everything in the relations of God and man must be and is determined by Him.[1]

But this problem of the Church thus begun and seen in the New Testament record of its first seventy years needs still more careful attention. We have to account not only for its beginning and early years, but also for its continuance to this day. Its history is capable of being followed from century to century, from country to country, up to the present time, when we see it settled in many places, and ever extending to fresh parts in the non-Christian world. Now all through these centuries there has been not a little essential continuity of method in all parts of the Christian community. There are in fact four chains stretching across the centuries which link the Church of to-day with that of the first ages.

First, there is the proclamation of the Christian message. In spite of differences of substance and method, something which has been regarded as a Christian Gospel has been proclaimed by means of various ministries through all the ages. Pioneers have gone from land to land with a message, a message about Christ, and this has been proclaimed and received and passed on everywhere. Second, there is the rite of Baptism, which has almost invariably accompanied the proclamation of the message of Christianity. This ordinance has been regarded and accepted as the occasion of initiation into Christianity, the proof of acceptance on the part of those who would become adherents. Third, there is the weekly worship on the first day. Christians have been

---

[1] Denney, *Jesus and the Gospel*, p. 101.

accustomed from the very first to meet together on this day and celebrate their Master's resurrection. There is scarcely anything more thoroughly capable of demonstration than this fact from the very rise of Christianity. It is incapable of explanation that companies of Jews should in time have ceased to meet together on the seventh day and at length transferred their gatherings to the first unless there had been sufficient cause for altering so ancient and honoured an observance. Fourth, there is the worship and fellowship in the Lord's Supper. Christians have been in the habit of meeting every week for the specific purpose of remembering their Master's death.

Now these four chains stretch across the centuries without the gap of a link and are found everywhere. How are they to be accounted for? Only in one way; as expressive of belief in and devotion to Jesus Christ on the part of the men and women who observed them. They were in use years before a line of our New Testament was written, so that our present records are not the cause of, but only an evidence for their existence. This identity of observance compels attention, and can only be explained by the relation of the people to Jesus Christ. These Christians believed in the death, resurrection, and Deity of their Master, and the ordinances were the outward expression and proof of their faith. The evidential value of preaching, Baptism, the Lord's Day, and the Lord's Supper is of the very first importance, and demands and warrants the closest attention.

There is, however, one remarkable fact connected with the existence of the Church of Christ which is an additional factor in the problem. Whenever Christianity has been faithfully proclaimed no compulsion has been used to lead men to believe in Christ, and, indeed, in all ages for the most part there has been no earthly advantage for men to become Christians. Not only so, but Christian profession has often meant social ostracism, persecution, and death. Both in regard to individual experience and to corporate life, opposition has had to be faced. Christianity has been checked and thwarted by civil and national authorities in almost every age. Whether in the Roman Empire or among barbaric hordes, attempts have been made to crush and destroy Christianity. But the result has ever been to make the Church stronger than before.

Now we have to account for this marvellous vitality, and we must have a sufficient explanation. If the law of causation obtains anywhere it surely applies here. Every effect must have its adequate cause. We have two problems to face which are, however, only parts of one still greater problem. The first is how to account for the New Testament attitude to Christ in the face of His death as a malefactor.

We do not always realise the nature of the issue here brought before us. Here is a young man scarcely thirty-three years of age, emerged from obscurity only for the brief space of three years, living during those years under the scorn of the world, which grew steadily in intensity and finally passed into hatred, and dying at the end the death of a malefactor: but leaving behind Him the germs of a worldwide community, the spring of whose vitality is the firm conviction that He was God manifest in the flesh. If anything human is obvious, it is obvious that this conviction was not formed and fixed without evidence for it of the most convincing kind.[1]

In the New Testament we find Jews with all their monotheistic passion actually regarding Jesus of Nazareth as equal to God the Father, and this well within

---

[1] Warfield, *The Lord of Glory*, p. 275.

twenty-five years of the time at which He was put to death as a criminal.[1] The fact is so striking and even startling that it is scarcely surprising that attempts should be made to modify or break its force. But it resists all such attempts, and remains one of the most convincing facts of early Church history.

What I cannot credit is, that by the time of the earliest Christian records His followers had already distorted and mistaken Him altogether so that the history of Christianity was built from the very foundation on a misunderstanding and a misrepresentation, behind which we must, after two thousand years, get back, if we are to have a real Christ and a genuine Christianity. "Back to Christ" is the watchword of theology in this generation; and I will repeat it with an enthusiasm born of a lifelong study of His words; but, when I go back to Him, I do not find a Christ who puts to shame the highest which His Church has taught about Him. He is different indeed—far more simple, actual, and human—yet in all that is most essential He is the same Son of God as for nineteen centuries has inspired the lives of the saints and evoked the worship of the world.[2]

The second part of the problem is the persistence of this view of Christ in relation to the Church all through the Christian centuries. It is no mere question, interesting and important as it is, of something happening nineteen centuries ago, as a fact of history; it is the question of the existence of a living, widespread, and ever-growing society, which has never been more alive than it is at present. And it is the existence of a society by means of one fact only, the persistent influence of Jesus Christ. The one bond which unites Christians together, the one secret of continuance in the Christian Church, is

[1] Fairbairn, *Christ in Modern Theology*, p. 377.
[2] Stalker, *The Christology of Jesus*, p. 122.

essentially a personal relation to Christ as a living Lord and Friend.

The most remarkable fact in the history of His religion is the continuous and ubiquitous activity of His person. He has been the permanent and efficient factor in its extension and progress. Under all its forms, in all its periods, and through all its divisions, the one principle alike of reality and unity has been and is devotion to Him. He is the Spirit that inhabits all the Churches, the law that rules the conscience and binds into awed and obedient reverence the saintly men who live within all the communions that bear His name.[1]

And so we challenge attention to the existence of the Christian Church as a proof of the uniqueness and supernatural power of the Person of Jesus Christ, for we are confident that it is impossible to account for the former apart from a belief in the latter. It is surely more probable that the Christian view of Christ arose out of the history than that the entire Christian Church should have invented a history to explain its foundation. The very divisions of the Christian Churches constitute an argument in support of this position, for this view of Christ is common to all the communities and underlies all their differences. How did the Church come by its faith in Christ? At least the history explains the faith, but the faith cannot fairly explain away the history.[2]

The connexion between Jesus and the Christian religion remains; and unless we are content to leave it entirely in the dark, we shall find ourselves compelled to raise the ulterior question which by this assumption is foreclosed. Granting that the figure in the Gospels is the product of the Church's faith, by what was that faith itself produced? The New Testament taken as a whole represents the most astonishing

[1] Fairbairn, *op. cit.*, p. 380.
[2] Garvie, *The Inner Life of Jesus*, p. 45.

outburst of intellectual and spiritual energy in the history of our race: by what was it evoked? Surely the probabilities are that some extraordinary reality—something quite unlike the rest of us—lies behind and explains all this.[1]

The problem of the Christian Church, then, has to be faced and solved. Its history requires some operative cause adequate to explain nineteen centuries of existence and progress. It is true that there have been other religions with millions of adherents, but it is also true that the existence and progress of the Church is something unique in history, to say nothing of the fact that Christianity has attracted to itself the profoundest thinkers of the human race, and is in no way hindered by the ever-advancing tide of human knowledge. The Church is, and ever has been, in such direct and constant relation to Christ that only His personality can explain its continued life and movement. The most extraordinary and inexplicable thing in the New Testament is the power of Jesus Christ of Nazareth over His early followers, and the most marvellous and astonishing thing in nineteen centuries of history is the power of His life over the members of the Christian Church.

---

[1] Denney, *Jesus and the Gospel*, p. 166.

CHAPTER X

THE GRACE OF CHRIST

———◄●►———

IT is only within comparatively recent years that attention has been given by scientific men to the fact and reality of Christian experience. Formerly it was either disregarded altogether or else set aside as too variable and unreliable to be worthy of serious notice. But this is no longer possible. The domain of science is being enlarged almost daily, and place is now being found for those experiences in human hearts and lives which accrue from the reception of Christ's teaching and the acknowledgment of His authority. They can be studied, and should be studied, for they are available for scientific investigation. There is such a thing as Christian experience, the precise and unique experience of those who are true followers of Christ, and this constitutes an argument of no mean weight and importance for the position for which we are now arguing.

We have already considered the evidence of the Church as a whole regarded as an objective fact of history and of present-day life. We must now seek to analyse what this means from the standpoint of the individual Christian who is a member of the Church—what it is that makes and keeps him a member of that society whose one bond of union is personal relationship to Christ. What constitutes this relationship—wherein lies its power over human lives?

It will be seen that this argument from experience is capable of being verified, quite apart from any question of the credibility of the Gospels or any proper appreciation of the various historical, philosophical, and critical arguments for Christ and Christianity. Not that we have any desire or intention to separate the Christ of History from the Christ of Experience, for the two are ultimately and inextricably united. But the verification of the Christ of Experience is possible apart from any elaborate discussion or intellectual conviction of the historical and theological grounds of belief in Christ. In its proper place and for its precise purpose this argument from experience is eminently worthy of consideration.

We can imagine some one approaching an old Christian of no great education or intellectual power, and putting before him the various arguments for Christianity based upon the Gospels, or the witness of the Church, or the results of Christianity in the world, and we can also imagine that old believer expressing his utter inability to understand and appreciate these arguments, and yet able to bear his own personal testimony to what Jesus Christ is to him as a living experience to-day. Now the question arises whether this argument from personal experience is valid. What is the claim of Christian experience? What does Christianity claim to-day for the individual?

A true follower of Jesus Christ will say that Christ has made an entire change in his life. He is conscious of a great difference between his past and his present. Old things have gone, new things have come. He is conscious of a burden removed, of a vision clarified; he knows something of what is meant by the Bible phrase, "the joy of salvation." Those who have not experienced this change may deny its reality, but not with any pretence to reason and fairness. We must take the testimony of reasonable, upright, and competent men when they tell us that Christ has made a difference to them.

Further, the true follower of Jesus Christ tells us that Christ has given a new direction to his life. Not only is the past different, the present also is changed. He is conscious of a new life, new powers, new principles, new aspirations, new hopes. He can say with literal truth, "Once I was blind; now I see," and "Old things have passed away; behold, all things have become new."

Yet again, the true follower of Jesus Christ tells us that Christ has provided a perfect satisfaction for his life. His mind is now at rest in the truth of Christ, his heart in the love of Christ, his conscience in the law of Christ, and his will in the grace of Christ. He is ready to be, to do, to suffer anything by reason of what Christ is to his soul. This consciousness of peace as he looks back over the past, of power as he considers the needs of the present, of hope as he surveys the possibilities of the future, are all very real, precious, and potent in his experience, and constitute the very life of his life.

This is the argument from Christian experience which is found in the New Testament, in all the centuries of Church history, and in the Christian life of to-day. Christ is real, Christ is precious, Christ is powerful, Christ is all. In our books of devotion Christ is the supreme object, in our hymns of praise and adoration Christ is the one theme, in the work of Christian missions Christ is the one subject underlying all differences of race, place, circumstance, temperament, and community. There is an irreducible minimum of experience, true of all genuine followers of Jesus Christ, and he who possesses it is perfectly conscious that Christ is a living reality.

In proof of this argument from Christian experience it would be possible to bring forward the evidence of representative men of all ages and Churches, such as Augustine, Bernard, Luther, Leighton, Bunyan, Wesley, and Wilberforce, but we will confine ourselves to one witness, a man who was formerly the ruthless persecutor of the Church of Christ, and who became one of the leading Christians of his age. We mean, of course, the Apostle Paul. He was never tired of bringing forward his own life as a testimony to the reality of Jesus Christ, and to the Gospel that he preached and lived. The witness of St. Paul is one of the chief arguments from the standpoint of Christian experience.

It will help us to appreciate this evidence the more if we recall something of what Saul the persecutor was as a man. He was a man of powerful intellect. He was a thinker, a man whose intellectual life showed unmistakable signs of his training at home, in Jerusalem, and as a member of the chief Council of the Jews. He was also a man of strong feeling. Intellect always influences feeling, and if the intellect is feeble the feelings will be feeble also. Saul of Tarsus could love in a way worthy of the name of love, and he could hate so as to make people fear his hatred. His feelings gave force to his purpose, emphasis to his words, decision to his actions. Still more, he was a man of intense conscientiousness. His training as a Jew had developed his scrupulosity and conscientiousness to a very high degree. Above all, he was a man of determined will. When intellect, feeling, and conscience combine to influence the will the real man is clearly seen. Saul had learned to hate Christ and Christianity. We are told that he persecuted them in Jerusalem, and went on his errand of hatred to the far-off city of Damascus. He was "exceedingly mad" against them, he "compelled them to blaspheme," he "breathed out threatenings and slaughters" against the Christians, he "made havoc of the Church," "dragging men and women to prison." This is the man of high capacity, expert knowledge, high culture, lofty intellect, intense virility, whom we wish to examine on behalf of Christian experience.

It is a simple matter of fact that the persecutor became convicted of his errors, and that this conviction led to an entire change of life and purpose. He soon began to love what he had formerly hated, and to preach the very Gospel that he had set out to destroy. How are we to account for this simple yet stupendous change? One of the keenest intellects of modern times, F. C. Baur of Tübingen, confessed that the conversion of Saul of Tarsus was an insoluble problem to him. "No psychological or dialectical analysis sufficiently explains the mystery of the act by which God revealed His Son to Saul." This admission of Baur remains unshaken to-day, and the problem of Saul's conversion still awaits solution by any other method than the one that he puts forth himself.

His conversion, however, was only the beginning of a new life. It is one thing to change, it is another to continue changed; and yet for twenty-five years his life was devoted to entirely opposite ends to those which had formerly been his experience. We have only to read his own testimony to what those years meant (2 Cor. xi.) as he preached, laboured, and suffered, to see the reality and the permanence of the change. It lasted. He

His conversion was only the beginning of a new life.

had everything to lose, and, humanly speaking, nothing
to gain by accepting Jesus Christ as his Master. Yet
amidst all the anxieties, toils, sufferings, and strain of
those twenty-five years he reveals a perfect satisfaction
with what had taken place on the way to Damascus and
with the living Christ whose servant he rejoiced to be.
In spite of his intensely strong individuality, he was
only an echo of Jesus Christ. From the moment of his
conversion his life was summed up in his own motto,
"To me to live is Christ."

Now if the Apostle's life of testimony to Christ is
true, his conversion must have involved a real change, a
deliberate break with his past. And if his conversion is
real, then Christ rose from the dead, and Christ is God.
The Apostle attributes everything to Christ. "Have I
not seen Jesus Christ our Lord?" He has the three
marks of the true witness—intelligence, candour, and
disinterestedness. And we are therefore warranted in
accepting his personal assurance that the revelation of
Jesus Christ produced in him that system of thought
and life which he calls his Gospel, and which is with us
to-day in the Christianity of the Epistles, and also in
that Christianity as reproduced in human life. We can
only account for his influence by means of his apostle-
ship and conversion. These in turn can only be explained by his own personal experience of Jesus Christ
as his Saviour and Lord.

Now this testimony of one man could be reproduced
in its essential features from the history of Christian
experience through the centuries. Christian biography
bears witness to the simple fact that, in whatever way
the experience called conversion comes, it brings with it
a definite break with the past, it gives an entirely new
aim to life, and it provides a perfect satisfaction in the

deep recesses of the soul. Wendell Phillips once made this reply in a coterie at Boston when some one told him that Jesus was amiable, but not strong. "Not strong?" replied he, "test the strength of Jesus by the strength of the men whom He has mastered." From the earliest records in the earliest books of the New Testament down to the latest records of the newest mission to the heathen the facts of Christian experience are to all intents and purposes essentially the same. Christ is living, Christ is real, Christ is powerful, Christ is precious—this is the one theme. Every conversion involves a distinct change, a definite consciousness of Christ, and a deep devotion to Him.

What is this but a moral miracle? And where else do we find it? It is not to be found in the pages of antiquity.

The old world knew nothing of conversion: instead of an *Ecce Homo* they had only some choice of Hercules.[1]

Nor is it to be found in the other great religious systems of to-day. The almost entire absence of the data of religious experience outside Christianity is a striking and significant fact. Professior William James acknowledges this in his study of religious experience.

The absence of strictly personal confessions is the chief difficulty to the purely literary student who would like to become acquainted with the inwardness of religions other than the Christian.[2]

How is it that these things are so? What is that type of saintliness which is found in the Christian Church and is not found elsewhere? It is best described as

[1] Carlyle, *Sartor Resartus*, book ii. ch. 10.
[2] James, *Varieties of Religious Experience*, p. 402.

Christlikeness, and the term at once suggests the reason why it is not found outside Christianity.

It is impossible to account for these experiences apart from personality. As they are realised in the personality of the Christian, so they proceed from the personality of Christ. No mere influence or impersonal force can explain the spiritual experiences of the Christian man. When we analyse them this is clearly seen. If we think of the forgiveness which leads to the break with the past, it is obvious that pardon comes from, and is received by, a person. If we think of the new aim and object which marks the Christian life, it is equally clear that nothing short of personal relations to a Person whose Will is henceforward the law of life can explain the force of this new trend in experience. And if we think of the inner satisfaction which is the deepest experience of the Christian, it seems impossible to believe that such satisfaction, covering as it does intellect, heart, conscience, and the whole inner moral being, can be derived from any source less than personal.

Religious thought is carried on in terms of personality, this being in the world of religion the one fundamental fact.[1]

And since personality is the source of religion, it is obvious that if that personality is not Christ's it is no one else's. We are therefore once again brought face to face with the fact of Christ in relation to Christian experience. It calls for close scrutiny and personal verification, and the more it is tested in this way, the more it will be found to crown the other arguments from history and reason. The more clearly, too, will it be seen that only on the assumption of a Divine Christ can Christian experience be explained.

[1] James, *op. cit.*, p. 491.

CHAPTER XI

THE INFLUENCE OF CHRIST

———————◆◆▶———————

THERE are many things in life about which we may be perfectly indifferent. Some are outside the sphere of our interest, others we can entirely ignore, while others again we may hold in solution without coming to any definite opinion. In politics it is not absolutely necessary for all to take sides, and in history there are many questions concerning men and movements as to which we may reserve our judgment. But the remarkable thing about Jesus Christ is that men have invariably had to take sides for or against Him. Indifference has always been impossible. Men have had to declare themselves either as His friends or as His foes. In considering the question with which we are now concerned, it is therefore valuable to inquire what those have thought of Christ who for any reason have not submitted their lives to Him. The testimony of opponents is often the very best evidence we can obtain of the reality of a life or a movement. It is to the subject of the influence of Christ, as witnessed both by His opponents and also by facts patent to everybody that we now call attention.

114

We have a remarkable chain of testimony to the impression made by Jesus Christ Himself during His earthly life. Among His contemporaries were those who, when sent to apprehend Him, came back without their prisoner, saying "Never man spake like this Man." Men of keen intellect like Pilate and Herod could not find any flaw in His conduct, while at His trial no two witnesses agreed together.

Subsequent testimony is in the same direction. Napoleon the Great said that Alexander, Cæsar, Charlemagne, and himself founded empires dependent upon force, while Jesus founded one on love, with the result that millions would die for Him.

I think I understand something of human nature, and I tell you all these were men, and I am a man. None else is like Him—Jesus Christ was more than man.[1]

Renan said that Jesus was the greatest religious genius that ever lived or will live, that His beauty is eternal, and His reign will never end.

Jesus is in every respect unique, and nothing can be compared with Him. Be the unlooked-for phenomena of the future what they may, Jesus will not be surpassed.[1]

Strauss calls Him—

The highest object we can possibly imagine with respect to religion, the being without whose presence in the mind piety is impossible.[1]

Rousseau says that—

If the life and death of Socrates are those of a philosopher, the life and death of Jesus Christ are those of a God.[1]

---

[1] Quoted in Ballard, *Miracles of Unbelief*, ch. viii.

These are but a few out of many more testimonies that could be adduced to the life and character of Jesus Christ, derived from the writings of those who, in spite of their encomiums, did not accept Him as their Saviour and God.

Scarcely less remarkable is the testimony of great scholars and thinkers to the work of Jesus Christ through the centuries as seen in Christianity. His work began in the place where He was crucified, among His enemies, and if there had been any untruth in the statements of His earliest disciples about Him it could easily have been shown and condemned. But His message made remarkable progress even among His inveterate foes, and it was not long before one of His disciples could say that the gospel had not only gone through Judæa and into Asia Minor, but into all the world. Not very much later we have the testimony of Tacitus, the Roman historian, to the progress of Christianity. Then in the second century comes the well-known evidence of Pliny concerning the early Christians who met week by week and worshipped Christ as God, and banded themselves together by an oath not to steal or to be untrue. Then arose the persecutions of the second and third centuries, with the boast of Tertullian that the more the Christians were persecuted, the more numerous they became—"the blood of the martyrs is the seed of the Church"—until at length, in the fourth and fifth centuries, we see the futile attempts of the Roman authorities to curb and crush Christianity, only to lead to the spread of it far and wide. Dr. Jowett, speaking of the century in which Christianity arose, says, "Could we have seen depicted the inner life of that brilliant period, we should have turned from it with loathing and disgust." And Renan, in words often quoted said, "Jesus Christ created a paradise out of the hell of Rome."[1]

As Christianity commenced, so it continued through the centuries, influencing men and States in proportion as it was allowed to be propagated in its purity and fulness. On the evidence of some of the greatest opponents of Christianity, it has surpassed all other religions in its remarkable power over human life. It has kept up with human growth and evolution through the ages, and it has shown itself to possess a capacity for cultivating holiness and developing character which has no equal in philosophy or religion in any part of the world. Mr. Lecky's words are well worth repeating—

The Platonist exhorted men to imitate God; the Stoic, to follow reason; the Christian, to the love of Christ. The later Stoics had often united their notions of excellence in an ideal sage, and Epictetus had even urged his disciples to set before them some man of surpassing excellence, and to imagine him continually near them; but the utmost the Stoic ideal could become was a model for imitation, and the admiration it inspired could never deepen into affection. It was reserved for Christianity to present to the world an ideal character, which through all the changes of eighteen centuries has inspired the hearts of men with an impassioned love; has shown itself capable of acting on all ages, nations, temperaments, and conditions; has been not only the highest pattern of virtue, but the strongest incentive to its practice; and has exercised so deep an influence that it may be truly said that the simple record of three short years of active life has done more to regenerate and soften mankind than all the disquisitions of philosophers and all the exhortations of moralists. This has indeed been the wellspring of whatever is best and purest in the Christian life. Amid all the sins and failings, amid all the

[1] See also Glover, *The Conflict of Religions in the Early Roman Empire*, chapters iv. and v.

priestcraft and persecution and fanaticism that have defaced the Church, it has preserved, in the character and example of its Founder, an enduring principle of regeneration.[1]

The testimony to the present work of Jesus Christ is not less real than it has been in the past. In the case of all the other great names of the world's history, the inevitable and invariable experience has been that the particular man is first a power, then only a name, and last of all a mere memory. Of Jesus Christ the exact opposite is true. He died on a cross of shame, His name gradually became more and more powerful, and He is the greatest influence in the world to-day. There is, as it has been well said, a fifth Gospel being written—the work of Jesus Christ in the hearts and lives of men and nations.

The present social status of men, women, and children is so familiar to us that we sometimes fail to realise what it was before Christ came. In the Roman world the father had absolute right over his children, to sell, to enslave, to kill them. It is Christianity that has made these atrocities impossible. Woman was the living chattel of her husband, as she is still in India and Africa. It is through Christianity that she has obtained a new status, and now in Christian countries "Home" receives its true and full meaning. The slavery of the Roman Empire was one of its most deep-seated features, and the power of master over slave was as absolute as it was often exercised with cruelty and ferocity. But Christianity proclaimed the universality and brotherhood of all men in Christ, and thereby struck at the root of slavery, and wherever the Gospel of Christ has had its way, slavery has been compelled to disappear. Then, too, the

---

[1] Lecky, *History of European Morals*, vol. ii., p. 8.

reality and purity of marriage are what they are to-day because of Christianity, while the blessings of humanitarianism, with the absence of cruelty, torture, and callousness, and the presence of hospitals, refuges, care for prisoners, kindness to animals, are all largely, and indeed mainly, attributable to the influence of Christ and His Gospel. The teaching of Christ about God, sin, redemption, holiness, love, has impressed, influenced, and inspired human life as nothing else has done and as, apparently, nothing else can do.[1]

Then, too, we are compelled to face the fact, the truly wonderful fact, of missionary enterprise. There are many things in which Christianity is like other religions, but the one element of unlikeness and uniqueness is its world-wide missions. Other religions may have their missions, but they lack the note of universality which is the most remarkable feature of Christian missions. Christianity, rising out of the narrowest of religions, is becoming the universal religion. Prompted by universal loyalty to Christ and universal love to man, missionaries have gone forth far and wide, backed by no earthly power, influenced by no earthly incentive, proclaiming the simple message of a personal Saviour, and wherever they have gone the results have been nothing short of stupendous. The general influence alone has been great in its formation of new literatures, new ideals, new philanthropies, while the transformations of men and races in Fiji, Uganda, New Zealand, Tierra del Fuego, are among the most noteworthy features of modern history. And when we study the lives of the missionaries who have gone forth on this errand of universal evangelisation we find among them the finest

[1] See Brace, *Gesta Christi*, chapters ii. to vii.

types of manhood. As we recall such names as Carey, Martyn, Livingstone, Patteson, Paton, Chalmers, Hudson Taylor, Hannington, Mackay, Pilkington, we realise that we are face to face with some of the most splendid and noble of characters. There is, in a word, no part of the modern outlook in which the power of Christianity is more evident than in the mission fields. A competent witness who has recently visited most of the great missionary centres of the world has given his testimony to the power of missionary effort.

I do not recall visiting a single country where I formed the impression that Christ and His cause are meeting with defeat. I do not remember having heard the voice of despair and pessimism from the leaders of the Christian hosts on any of these continents. True it is that I have visited fields where the forces of our Lord seem to be hard pressed; but taking the world as a whole, I may say that victory is being achieved.[1]

When, therefore, we think of the moral and social achievements of Christianity in the past, especially in regard to women, children, and slaves; when we think of its influence to-day both at home and in other lands; when we recall its power compared with that of other religions in regard to deliverance from sin, power for holy living, and incentives to individual and collective progress, we fearlessly challenge all attempts to find anything like it, or to account for this influence apart from a belief in Jesus Christ as Lord and God. All the great modern nations of the world date their history from the birth of Christ, and even the sceptic testifies to Christ by the date of his letters. It is Christianity alone which gives to the Western world its vast superiority

[1] Address, July 1908, by Mr. J. R. Mott. *Cf.* his *Modern World Movements*, p. 17. See also a fine statement by Dr. J. H. Moulton, *Hibbert Journal*, vol. vii. p. 665 (July 1909).

over the Eastern, and its irresistible impulse to progress. Japan in particular bears its indirect but very real testimony to the power of Christianity, for the main secret of Japan's metamorphosis and marvellous development is the adoption of Western ideals which have largely sprung from Christianity. East and West unite in their testimony to the influence of Jesus Christ.

I shall take, first, the well-known saying of Keshub Chunder Sen, one of the most remarkable and representative figures of modern times. "If you wish to secure that allegiance and attachment of India, it must be through spiritual influence and moral suasion." And such indeed has been the case in India. You cannot deny that your hearts have been touched, conquered, and subjugated by a superior power. That power, need I tell you, is Christ. It is Christ who rules British India, and not the British Government. England sent out a tremendous moral power in the life and character of the mighty prophet, to conquer and to hold this vast Empire. . . . Take now what Max Göhre in his remarkable volume, *Drei Monate Fabrik-Arbeiter*, tells us of the inner thought of that formidable new democracy that is growing up in modern Germany, alienated not only from the present social order, but from all conventional religious belief and communion. After drawing the darkest picture of the lapse from all definite Christian belief of the workmen in the Chemnitz factory in which he laboured, he says, "One thing only has remained in all of them—esteem and reverence of Jesus Christ."[1]

Nor can we overlook the evidence of Christ's influence, as men are brought face to face with the deepest problem of life. What are we to say of the problem of human sin? Call it what we like, the fact by any other name would be as bad. Where can we find the power to deliver man from evil, to overcome the evil principle within, and to give the conscience rest and peace amidst

[1] Cairns, *Christianity in the Modern World*, p. 16.

the burdens of life? Cotter Morison in his *Service of Man*, which on its publication twenty-two years ago was spoken of as the most powerful attack on Christianity during that generation,[1] frankly admits that there is no remedy for a bad heart, that society has a right to extirpate the hardened criminal, and to prevent him from leaving a progeny as bad as himself.[2] There is no good news in this for the outcast, the depraved, the abandoned, the hopeless. To tell such people that they are to be extirpated is to confess the ghastly failure to deal with sin. Nor can education, or philosophy, or even social reform cope with this gigantic power of evil. Yet thousands and millions to-day, as in all ages, are testifying to the power and glory of Christianity in dealing with their sin and wickedness. These are facts which stand the test of examination and carry their own conclusion to all who are willing to learn.

What, too, shall we say about human weakness, the inability to live righteous lives, the constant struggle and defeat in the face of what seems to be omnipotent foes? Science, with all its discoveries and glories during the past century, has no word of hope for the individual. It may be true, as Darwin says, that all organised beings are slowly advancing towards perfection, but meanwhile what joy or comfort is this to the individual who longs to live a holy life, and who finds himself powerless to resist the forces within him and around him? The old question still awaits an answer—

> "Canst thou not minister to a mind diseased,
> Pluck from the memory a rooted sorrow?"

---

[1] *Athenæum*, Jan. 29, 1887.
[2] J.C. Morison, *Service of Man*, pp. 293–5.

And there is no answer apart from Jesus Christ.

What, too, are we to say about the unrest of soul as we attempt to peer into the future? Here again science has nothing to say. Science has inspired us with wonderful hope during the last fifty years, until there seems scarcely any limit to human discoveries and inventions, and yet in the midst of all this hopefulness there never has been a time when men have been more hopeless or uncertain about the future. The testimony of Tyndall to the futility of materialism,[1] the tacit admission of Huxley in his invention of the word "agnostic," and the pessimism of Thomas Hardy are illustrations of the utter powerlessness of philosophy, science, education, culture, progress to deal with the deepest problems of human life. And yet all the while many and many a simple-hearted life is finding in Jesus Christ the secret of deliverance from sin, the guarantee against moral weakness, and the inspiration of an immortal hope.

It is, of course, true that Mohammed, Buddha, and Confucius have founded religions that now possess millions of followers, but the patent fact is that these religions are not making progress among the most enlightened and civilised races, while Christianity is gradually extending its boundaries and compelling the attention of the best thought of the world. How is it that the other religions are either stationary or else retreating before the advance of knowledge, while Christianity is ever pushing forward into fresh enterprises of thought and action all over the world? What was it in the personality of Jesus Christ that accounts for His influence on mankind in the past, and what *is* it that accounts for His growing influence on the most highly

---

[1] *Belfast Address*, Preface, p. 36.

civilised nations to-day? How is it that during the nineteen centuries of Christianity in the world, with all the progress of human thought and life, not a single new ethical idea has been discovered outside the teaching of Jesus Christ? How is it that a religion emanating almost entirely from a narrow and obscure people like the Jews should possess the completest ethical ideal that the world knows, and one capable of ever extending application to all circumstances and conditions of human life?

When Jesus Christ left this earth He told His disciples that after His departure they should do greater works than He had done, and the centuries of Christianity have borne out the truth of this statement. Works greater in kind have been done—are being done. Jesus Christ is doing more wonderful things to-day than ever He did when on earth, redeeming souls, changing lives, transforming characters, exalting ideals, inspiring philanthropies, and making for the best, truest, and highest in human life and progress.

We are therefore justified in calling attention to the influence of Christ through the ages as one of the greatest, most direct, and most self-evident proofs that Christianity is Christ, and that Christ has to be accounted for. It is impossible to consider this question solely as one of history; it touches life at every point to-day.

We have not solved, we have not even stated and defined, the problem as to the Person of Christ when we have written the life of Jesus, for that problem is raised even less by the Gospels than by Christ's place and function in the collective history of man. . . . The very essence of the matter is that the Gospels do not stand alone, but live, as it were, embosomed in universal history. And in that history Christ plays a part much more remarkable and much less compatible with common manhood than the part Jesus plays in the history of His own age and people. And we have not solved, or even apprehended, any one of the problems connected with His person until we have resolved the mystery of the place He has filled and the things He has achieved in the collective life of man.[1]

Who and what must Jesus Christ be to have effected all this? Surely we are compelled to admit at least His uniqueness. And when we have done this we are bound to go further and inquire as to the secret and explanation of this uniqueness. Why should Jesus, the Jewish peasant of Nazareth, have become the Founder of a religion which has shown and is showing its power to become a universal religion? The only adequate explanation of His work is the Christian explanation of His Person—He was God manifest in the flesh.

[1] Fairbairn, *The Philosophy of the Christian Religion*, p. 13.

CHAPTER XII

THE VIRGIN-BIRTH OF CHRIST[1]

———◆◆►———

ALTHOUGH the Virgin-Birth is not strictly an evidence of the Divine Person of Christ, but simply the New Testament explanation of the earthly origin and appearance of His Person, it seems necessary to include a consideration of it in the present discussion. The prominence given to the question is one of the most obvious facts of recent theological thought. While, therefore, the purpose of this book would have been fully served without any discussion of the Virgin-Birth, the attention devoted to that problem for several years past is so thoroughly indicative of a general attitude to Christianity on the part of many minds, that it may be well to state the Christian view and to give reasons for adhering to the New Testament teaching. Without concentrating attention on particular arguments, it is proposed to adduce several reasons which singly and cumulatively support a belief in the truth of the Virgin-Birth.

[1] This chapter appeared in substance in the *Bible Record* (New York, U.S.A.), for December 1907, as one of a series of papers issued in connection with a course of lectures on the Virgin-Birth of Christ by Dr. Orr, which have since been published in book form in *The Virgin-Birth of Christ*. References to and quotations from the paper appear on pp. 284 ff. of Dr. Orr's book.

Starting from the most obvious position, the Virgin-Birth is the account of our Lord's introduction to earth which is found in the New Testament. The chapters in Matthew and Luke present this view, and no other is fairly deducible from the records as we now possess them. We are therefore on sure ground in arguing that at least the authenticity of the first and third Gospels in their present integrity is involved in the denial of the Virgin-Birth. If this is not a fact, our Gospels can hardly retain the position they have had for centuries, at any rate so far as the early chapters are concerned. And even though the rest of the Gospels may conceivably be spared, their value must necessarily be greatly weakened by the removal of these early chapters.

There is no certain warrant on purely literary and textual grounds for separating these chapters from the rest of the Gospels of which they form a part. The brevity and reserve which characterise the chapters in relation to the Virgin-Birth are very noteworthy. There are only two verses in Luke's account which actually deal with the Virgin-Birth, though, of course, the whole narrative is instinct with the idea. Further, there are no valid arguments based on textual criticism that would lead us to separate these chapters from the rest of the Gospel. Still more, the claim made by Luke in his preface to have "carefully traced everything accurately from the first" is a strong argument in favour of their authenticity. Nor can we disregard Luke's medical training, his close association with St. Paul, and the significant reference in Gal. iv. 4 to our Lord being born of a woman. Even if this be not a subtle allusion to the uniqueness implied in the Virgin-Birth, we may fairly argue for the authenticity of the story from all that we know of Luke personally and from his association with the great Apostle of the Gentiles. Not least of all, the clear independence of the genealogies given by Matthew and Luke is an unmistakable proof of the genuineness of these chapters.

We find another support for belief in the Virgin-Birth in the universal belief of the Church in all ages. All recent criticism tends to push back the dates of the Gospels well into the first century, and they thus become strong witnesses for the belief of the Church of that day. It is also a simple matter of historical fact that from the time of Ignatius the Virgin-Birth has been held by the Church, and has for centuries been enshrined in the great historic creeds. Surely this would count for a great deal even after making all possible allowance for the uncritical ages of the Church. The early date of the Gospels leaves no adequate time for the growth of myth and legend or for the apotheosis of Christ by enthusiastic disciples. The early reception and universal acceptance by the Christian Church of the idea of the Virgin-Birth is one of the greatest historical problems unless it has been based upon simple fact.

The chief support for the doctrine is, however, the necessity of accounting for the uniqueness of the life of Jesus. The fact of this uniqueness, as we have seen, is "writ large" on the Gospels and the rest of the New Testament. It constitutes the problem of the ages, and has hitherto defied solution in any other way except by the Christian explanation. Now it may fairly be contended that such a unique life demands a unique origin and entrance into the world. We have to be told when and how this supernatural life began on earth. If we believe that in the Person of Jesus Christ God was manifest in the flesh, we may point to the Virgin-Birth as at least a satisfactory way of accounting for that

Divine coming into human life. As it is impossible to reduce the person of Jesus to the limits of ordinary humanity, we work back from His uniqueness to discover some explanation of His method of entrance upon human conditions. Let us suppose Jesus to be very God, and the Virgin-Birth becomes at least credible.

Our belief in the doctrine is supported by the consideration that no other adequate explanation is forthcoming as an alternative. The doctrine continues to hold the field as accounting for the entrance of Jesus into our humanity. Every effect must have its adequate cause, and the life of Christ finds no other cause or explanation than that of the Virgin-Birth, so far as His earthly origin is concerned. Besides, the Virgin-Birth seems to include and combine all the elements which were required for the human life of the Messiah.

(*a*) The Messiah was to be the legal heir of Joseph. Betrothal gave the legal status of wedlock (Deut. xxii. 23, 24), and in such phrases as "Mary thy wife" (Matt. i. 20), "His father David" (Luke i. 32), we see the fulfilment of this requirement in the Person of Jesus, the Son of Mary, the betrothed wife of Joseph, the heir of Solomon.

(*b*) The Messiah was to be born of a virgin, or at least of a young woman. Whether Isaiah vii. 14 is to be rendered by "virgin" or "young woman," a Messianic application of the passage seems clear, and coming midway between the "seed of the woman" (Gen. iii. 15), and "born of a woman" (Gal. iv. 4), it certainly points to His human parentage on the maternal side.

(*c*) The Messiah was to be the Son of God. Another Messianic passage is Isaiah ix. 6, where the Child with the four or five names is clearly some one far beyond any human personality, and in the light of Luke i. 32,

35, and ii.11, it is impossible not to see in these passages the unique Divine Sonship of the Messiah as realised in Jesus the Son of Mary.

(*d*) The Messiah was to be a perfect sacrifice for sin. The Passover and other offerings required by the Mosaic law pointed forward to something yet to come, to the blood which spoke "better things than that of Abel"; and in view of such passages as 1 Peter i. 19 we can readily see how the sinless and spotless Person of Jesus was the complete fulfilment of these typical anticipations.

Now, when these four historical requirements are considered separately and together, they are seen to be fulfilled by Him whom the Church believes to have been "conceived of the Holy Ghost, born of the Virgin Mary." There is no other personage in history in whom all these four requirements are blended, united, correlated and fulfilled. We have a right to demand an alternative before giving up the universal belief of centuries.

Our reluctance to yield the question of the Virgin-Birth is confirmed by a consideration of the attitude of mind on the part of many who deny it. In general, the denial is due to the prevalence of belief in a doctrine of evolution. Now, whatever may be said of this doctrine in the spheres of natural and mental science, we are still without proof that morality can be accounted for by it, much more that human self-consciousness and self-determination are explicable thereby. Above all, we are faced with the fact that Jesus Christ cannot be explained in terms of evolution; the records of His life and extraordinary influence conclusively disprove the theory in His case, and in view of this great exception we have a right to say that if evolution cannot account for His personality as Man, it may well be unable to account for His

Conceived of the Holy Ghost, born of the Virgin
Mary.

human origin. If a Divine intervention was necessary to account for the Man Christ Jesus, it may have been equally necessary for His earthly origin. At least there is no *a priori* reason why this should not be the case.

There is, however, a special reason for being suspicious of present-day denials of the Virgin-Birth. They are connected with a phase of modern philosophy which substitutes for a Divine Incarnation in the Person of Christ a Divine Immanence in creation, and will allow only such Immanence in Christ as we find in nature and in man. Further, this philosophy substitutes ideas for facts, and dissipates the historic personality of Jesus in ideas which are to have for us the value of God and His truth. Now it is manifestly easy to surrender the Virgin-Birth if there has been no Incarnation and no historical revelation of God in Christ, but granted the historical appearance at a particular period of Jesus Christ as Messiah and Redeemer, it is obvious that no mere natural and human considerations, and certainly no mere ideas, will account for Him. It is an unquestioned historical fact that from the time of Cerinthus, who was the first to deny the Virgin-Birth, denial of this has often led to the rejection of the Incarnation itself.

The historic Person of Jesus as Messiah and Saviour as stated in the former chapters has still to be explained, and all attempts to solve the problem apart from a Divine Incarnation have utterly failed. It is futile to say that belief in the Virgin-Birth is due to Jewish ideas, while at the same time the one Old Testament text that looks in that direction (Isa. vii. 14) is denied. If that passage is not to be used in support of the doctrine, then there is no Old Testament anticipation whatever, and certainly nothing in Jewish literature of the time of Christ to account for the doctrine. Nor is there any

proof that any such expectation prevailed among Alex-
andrian Jews as represented by Philo. Again, there is no
trace of Oriental influence on Christianity which would
account for a belief in the Virgin-Birth. The chapters in
the Gospels are essentially Jewish in characteristics, and
not only is there no trace of any such contact of Oriental ideas with primitive Christianity as would suffice for
the doctrine of the Virgin-Birth, but still more, the
hostility of early Christianity to other forms of thought
would almost certainly have prevented any such influence if it had been forthcoming. The argument from
incarnations as believed in India to-day is not to the
point, because there is no real trace of any early contact
between Christianity and India, and also because these
Indian incarnations have no virgin-birth associated with
them. They are witnesses to the doctrine of a Divine
Immanence, but nothing more.[1]

The one rock on which all these non-miraculous theories are shattered is the historic Person of the Man
Christ Jesus. He has to be accounted for. The effect
demands a sufficient cause, and the Virgin-Birth alone
gives this adequate explanation of the mode of entrance
upon His earthly life.

If it be asked why this doctrine was not made prominent in the early Church and put in the forefront of
apostolic preaching, the reply is obvious. There was no
need of it. Attention was rightly concentrated on the
resurrection of Jesus and the Divine claim involved in
that. In other words, it was the unique Personality
rather than the mode of His earthly appearance that
formed the gospel. We can see this by a simple illustration. The Apostles preached the Divine forgiveness of

[1] See Tisdall, *Mythic Christs and the True*, for a discussion on the supposed
connection of Christianity with Eastern faiths and cults.

sins in Christ instead of proclaiming the Godhead as a Trinity revealed in Father, Son, and Holy Ghost. By so doing the hearers would be led through the avenue of personal experience to a spiritual assurance concerning Christ which no intellectual discussion could either give or take away. But on the basis of this personal experience the early Christians would inevitably seek some intellectual explanation, and thus from their personal consciousness of Jesus Christ in His redeeming power they would rise to a distinction between Him and the Father which virtually carried with it an essential distinction such as is now involved in the doctrine of the Trinity. We can see that by the time of 2 Corinthians (xiii. 14) the Christian doctrine of the Godhead as Triune was perfectly clear. In the same way, the doctrine of the Virgin-Birth would in due course give the early Christians the needed and adequate explanation of the mode of the appearance of Christ, and we know by the date of Luke's Gospel that the doctrine was then fully known and accepted. The preaching of the fact of the Incarnation rather than the mode is the true method of presenting the Gospel; first what Christ is, and only then how He came to be what He is. In these considerations of the true perspective of Christian teaching we may rightly explain the silence of St. Paul and St. John. There was no need of the Virgin-Birth for evangelistic purposes, but only for the intellectual instruction of Christian people. Adequate reasons could be given for silence on this point in the earliest years of the Church, but to argue from this silence to a disbelief, or at any rate to an ignorance of the doctrine on the part of the early Christians, is not only in the highest degree precarious, but is really contradictory of the facts associated with the early date of Luke's Gospel.

From all this it will have been seen that the Virgin-Birth cannot be viewed alone or discussed merely on its historical evidences. It must be considered in the light of our impression of Christ and His revelation. In other words, our decision will virtually depend upon our theological and philosophical presuppositions concerning Jesus Christ. As Illingworth rightly says—

It is impossible to approach any complex problem without presuppositions; and doubly so a problem that not only involves physical, moral, and spiritual elements all combined, but is also of supreme personal interest, of one kind or another, to all who approach it, and touches human nature to the quick. Indeed, it is not too much to say that the controversies waged over the Gospel history are entirely concerned with the presuppositions of the respective combatants. The Gospels considered as documents that have come down to us are the same facts for all alike. It is over their interpretation that issue is joined, and this interpretation is determined by our presuppositions.[1]

Even if it were possible to satisfy every one on the historical and critical problems connected with the early dates and integrity of the first and third Gospels, we should not have settled the question. The decision depends on something far deeper than scholarship. It turns on our view of the Person of Christ, whether or not He is Divine, supernatural, miraculous. Attention must be concentrated on this point. The ultimate solution of a belief in the Virgin-Birth lies in the answer to the question, "What think ye of Christ?"

We therefore see no reason for rejecting the testimony of the Gospels and the witness of the whole Church to the Virgin-Birth. If the narratives of the Gospels are not true, they are a deliberate fiction; there is no other

[1] Illingworth, *Reason and Revelation*, pp. 88, 89.

alternative. And if the Church has been mistaken throughout the centuries, it is certainly the greatest, most widespread, and most persistent delusion that has ever been known. Two almost insuperable difficulties appear in this connection: (1) How did the idea of the Virgin-Birth arise so soon if it was not based on fact? (2) How were the narratives of the Gospels accepted so early and universally if they were not historical?

The Person of Christ must, therefore, be accounted for. A sinless Man is a moral miracle, and inasmuch as mind must have an organism by which to express itself, there is no valid reason for not accepting a physical miracle. We approach the Virgin-Birth with the definite belief in Jesus Christ as God to which we have come on independent grounds, and our acceptance of the truth of the Virgin-Birth is thus mainly due to our prior belief in the Godhead of Christ. To quote Dr. Stanton—

Believing in the indissoluble union between God and man in Jesus Christ, the miraculous birth of Jesus seems to us the only fitting accompaniment of this union, and, so to speak, the natural expression of it in order of outward facts.[1]

The ultimate decision will perhaps only be arrived at by settling the question as to what Jesus came into the world to do. If the one thing that man needs is illumination, then ideas will suffice, and no Divine Incarnation is necessary, but if there is such a thing as sin in the world, we must predicate a Divine, sinless Redeemer to deal with it. For such a Redeemer the only adequate explanation, so far as His earthly origin is concerned, is the ancient belief of the Church Universal that He was "conceived of the Holy Ghost, born of the Virgin Mary."

[1] Stanton, *The Jewish and the Christian Messiah*, p. 376.

CHAPTER XIII

THE MEANING OF CHRIST

———◆●▸———

FACTS can never be properly appreciated until an endeavour is made to penetrate behind them to their meaning. We have now reached the point when an attempt must be made to discover the meaning of all this emphasis on Christ. We have considered His character as perfect and sinless, His claim to Divine authority over mankind, His death as an atonement for sin, His resurrection as the demonstration of His Divine life, His Gospels as faithful records of His earthly manifestations, His Church as the perpetual testimony to His saving power, His grace as witnessed to by His devoted followers, His influence as acknowledged by some of His greatest foes. But what does it all mean? Why do we lay such stress on the Fact, the Person, and the Work of Christ?

The answer is, because Christ is before everything else a revelation of God. This, and nothing short of it, is the one and complete explanation of Christ. The idea of God is the dominating idea in all religions, and the idea of Christ as the Revealer of God is the dominating idea in Christianity. The supreme message of Christianity is, "There is one God and one Mediator between

136

God and man, Himself man, Jesus"; one God, and one unique Mediator as the personal Revealer of God to man. No one can doubt that this is the meaning of the place given to Christ in the New Testament.

The Name of Christ is found everywhere therein, and always in connection with His personal revelation of God. It meets our gaze at all points, and proclaims with no uncertain sound that to us men God has revealed Himself in Christ Jesus, that for us, for religion, for Christianity, for salvation, for life, Christ is God. The disciple's question addressed to Christ, "Show us the Father," is at once an admission of his own need and a confession of his belief that Christ could supply it; and the relation of Jesus Christ to God is set forth in the New Testament with no uncertain sound. "All things are delivered to Me of My Father" (Matt. xi. 27). "He that hath seen Me hath seen the Father" (John xiv. 9). He is the image of the invisible God, the effulgence of His glory (Heb. i. 3). Jesus Christ, divine and human, is for all time and for all men the final, complete, and sufficient manifestation of God.

The unchangeable sum of Christianity is the message: *The Word was God, and the Word became flesh.* This being so, it is clear that Christianity is not essentially a law for the regulation of our conduct; not a philosophy for the harmonious co-ordination of the facts of experience under our present forms of thought; not a system of worship by which men can approach their Maker in reverent devotion. It offers all these as the natural fruit of the Truth which it proclaims in the Incarnation and Resurrection of Christ. But Christ Himself, His person and His Life, in time and beyond time, and not any scheme of doctrine which He delivered, is the central object and support of faith.[1]

---

[1] Westcott, *The Gospel of Life*, p. 100.

This, and this alone, constitutes essential Christianity. Whatever men may find and emphasise in Christ, His Sonship, His Messiahship, His Teaching, His Manhood —while these are all included in the essence of Christianity, they do not exhaust it. Christianity as Christ conceived of it transcends all these different aspects by embracing them in the one supreme and dominant truth of His personal revelation of God. The essential fact is that He brings God to man in order that He may bring men to God.

Man's greatest, deepest need is God, and union and communion with Him. "Thou hast made us for Thyself, O Lord, and our heart is restless until it rests in Thee." Personality can only be satisfied with personality, and man's personality can never be satisfied with any personality short of God's. Now this fellowship with God, Christ came to reveal and mediate, and it is the bare truth to say that He reveals and mediates it as none else does or ever has done.

We may argue, first, directly from the fact of Christ Himself—His life, His teaching, and especially His consciousness—as the greatest and most significant fact in the world, and so our best proof of the existence of God in the full Christian sense. This seems to me, even from the side of pure argument, the most decisive proof. The argument goes upon the simple assumption that, if we are ever to discern the real nature of the ultimate world-ground, our best light must come from the greatest and most significant facts. For myself, I have no doubt that Christ is the most significant of all facts known to us, and, therefore, the best basis for direct and decisive inference to the nature of the world-ground. The argument does not at all go, it should be noticed, upon any assumption of the arbitrary authority of Jesus, but simply upon the significance of what He is. Any authority consequently given Him must be based wholly upon what He is in fact found to be. I count the fact of Christ, the greatest of all proofs of a completely satisfying God—the proof most powerful to produce conviction in the mind of a man who has himself come ot full moral self-consciousness.[1]

In Christ, we see what God is, both in His personal character and also in His relation to us. He is that Love, Wisdom, Righteousness, Grace for which we crave, while in Him we are enabled to understand and experience what God wills us to be. This doctrine meets our deepest needs as nothing else can.

> "The very God! Think, Abib; dost thou think?
> *So*, the All-Great, were the All-Loving too—
> So, through the thunder comes a human voice,
> Saying, 'O heart I made, a heart beats here!
>
> .   .   .   .   .   .
>
> And thou must love Me who hast died for thee.' "

This is *the* Gospel, the good news. He was God manifest in the flesh, and came to this earth "that He might bring us to God." It is this that makes Christ central and dominant in every life that receives Him, winning trust, redeeming from sin, eliciting devotion, and inspiring hope. It is because He is God manifest, God entering into human life, God meeting human need.

The most important thing for the man who is to submit himself to God is surely that he should be absolutely certain of the reality of God, and Jesus does establish in us, through the fact of His personal life, a certainty of God which covers every doubt. When once He has attracted us by the beauty of His Person, and made us bow before Him by its exalted character, then even amid our deepest doubts, the Person of Jesus will remain present with us as a thing incomparable, the

---

[1] King, *The Seeming Unreality of the Spiritual Life*, p. 202.

most precious fact in history, the most precious fact our life contains.[1]

But, it is said, the Person of Christ is a mystery—the union of God and Man in one Person is beyond our comprehension. True, but is this a reason for setting it aside altogether? Beyond comprehension is not necessarily beyond apprehension, and apprehension is a reality and provides a sufficiency which covers most of the essential things of life. Wherever deity and humanity meet there is—there must be—mystery, and we cannot therefore be surprised that since they meet in Jesus Christ as they do nowhere else, the element of mystery has always been realised.

The Person of Christ is exactly the point in the Christian religion where the intellect feels overwhelmed by mysteries it cannot resolve, yet where Christian experience finds the factors of its most characteristic qualities, and the Church the truth it has lived by and is bound to live for.[2]

The solution of the problem has been attempted in almost every age, but without success. It is easy to cut the gordian knot by denying one or other of the conditions of the problem—by rejecting either the Deity or the Humanity. This at once resolves the mystery, but it also leaves the facts concerning Christ a greater problem than ever. These facts have to be explained, and cannot be set aside simply because they are mysteries. When all allowance has been made, there remains an irreducible minimum of fact about the historic Christ which calls for attention and explanation. We cannot get rid of facts by describing them as inexplicable. The true hu-

[1] Herrmann, *Communion with God*, p. 97.
[2] Fairbairn, *The Philosophy of the Christian Religion*, p. 5.

manity of Jesus Christ is a patent fact of the New
Testament record, and yet the way in which His life
transcended humanity is equally patent. The supreme
idea that runs through the Gospel story is the consciousness that Jesus Christ is more than man. Whether
we read of the Virgin-Birth, the Miracles, the Character, the Death, or the Resurrection, it cannot be doubted
that the writers intend us to obtain the impression that
Jesus Christ was a unique manifestation of God. Dr.
Denney points out this in referring to the Virgin-Birth—

It provides a way of expressing the assurance that the life
of Christ is throughout Divine. If He was Son of God at all,
He did not begin to be so at any given age. . . . He never was
anything else. This is the truth guarded by the Virgin-Birth.[1]

It is impossible to reconstruct the life of Jesus on a
purely natural, historic, and non-mysterious basis. Those
who attempt to do so have confessedly no new historical
facts to deal with, no new contemporary documents to
put against our Gospels. The supernatural element in
Christ and Christianity remains, and demands attention.

I start from the fact, which appears to me to be as certain
as anything in history, that extraordinary phenomena happened in connection with the life of Christ and the ministry
of His Apostles, and happened on a large scale. The most
decisive witness on this head is St. Paul, who speaks not only
from his own experience, but from that of his immediate
contemporaries and associates. . . . These forces of which the
Apostle is conscious had their rise, as he knows and the
whole Church knows, in the life and work of Christ, which
set the train in motion. . . . The inference backwards that we
draw from the writings of St. Paul is abundantly confirmed

[1] Denney, article, "Jesus Christ," Hastings' *Bible Dictionary*, One Volume
Edition.

by every document that criticism can distinguish bearing upon the life of Christ. We cannot help seeing that not only St. Paul and the authors of these documents, named or unnamed, but the whole body of Christian opinion at the time, agreed in assuming, not merely that extraordinary things happened in connection with the Person of Jesus, but that His Person was itself extraordinary and transcendent, something beyond the measures of common humanity.[1]

So that when we read the Gospels and the testimony of the Apostles we are face to face with the belief not only and merely of the particular writers, but with that of the whole Christian community of which they were the exponents and for which they wrote.[2]

But beyond this and arising out of it is the supernatural element in the Christianity of the centuries. After destructive criticism has done all its work on the Gospels, the problem still remains. The Church, as we have already seen, has to be accounted for, the community of all races drawn and held together through the ages by the love of Christ's Name. This, too, is a supernatural fact, which is characterised by mystery and needs an explanation. Whether, then, we think of Christ or of the Church, we are in the presence of the supernatural, and therefore of mystery, and we maintain the utter impossibility of resolving the mystery on natural grounds. If we are to reject Christ because He is mysterious, we shall inevitably find ourselves face to face with other facts for which there is no explanation. The history of nineteen centuries becomes an insoluble enigma, and man is left absolutely alone without God, and without the satisfaction of those needs which are as clamant to-day as they have ever been.

[1] Sanday, *Expository Times*, vol. xx. p. 157.
[2] Warfield, *The Lord of Glory*, pp. 133, 144.

The only possible explanation of Christ and Christianity is that He was God revealed in human form. His uniqueness in relation to God makes the Christian doctrine of the Incarnation the only adequate explanation of His personality and work. It is utterly impossible to hold to a merely human Christ. The Christ who proclaims God, who forgives sin, who unites men to God, who is and has ever been honoured and worshipped in the Church, is the only satisfying solution of the problem of how God and man may be brought together, and man's life find its full realisation and satisfaction.

Grant that Jesus was really God, in a word, and everything falls orderly into its place. Deny it, and you have a Jesus and a Christianity on your hands both equally unaccountable: and that is as much as to say that the ultimate proof of the deity of Christ is just—Jesus and Christianity. If Christ were not God, we should have a very different Jesus and a very different Christianity. And that is the reason that modern unbelief bends all its energies in a vain effort to abolish the historical Jesus and to destroy historical Christianity. Its instinct is right, but its task is hopeless. We need the Jesus of history to account for the Christianity of history. And we need both the Jesus of history and the Christianity of history to account for the history of the world. The history of the world is the product of that precise Christianity which has actually existed, and this Christianity is the product of the precise Jesus which actually was. To be rid of this Jesus we must be rid of this Christianity, and to be rid of this Christianity we must be rid of the world-history which has grown out of it. We must have the Christianity of history and the Jesus of history, or we leave the world that exists, and as it exists, unaccounted for. But so long as we have either the Jesus of history or the Christianity of history we shall have a divine Jesus.[1]

---

[1] Warfield, *op. cit.*, p. 278.

CHAPTER XIV

THE VERIFICATION OF CHRIST

————◄●►————

A WELL-KNOWN American scholar in his early ministry many years ago preached a course of sermons on the Resurrection, in which he stated and tested the various arguments to the fullest extent of his power. There was present in his audience an eminent lawyer, the head of the legal profession in the city. He listened to the preacher Sunday by Sunday as he marshalled proofs, weighed evidence, considered objections, analysed the stories of the Gospels, and stated the case for the Resurrection. At length the conclusion was drawn by the preacher that Christianity must be true since Jesus was raised from the dead. At the close of the last sermon the lawyer went to see the minister and said, "I am a lawyer; I have listened to your statement of the case; I consider it incontrovertible, but *this case demands a verdict*. This is no mere intellectual conflict; there is life in it. If Jesus Christ rose from the dead, His religion is true, and we must submit to it." The lawyer was as good as his word and became a Christian.

The same is true of our present subject; the case demands a verdict. It is no mere question of dialectic, no topic of argumentative discussion only, no matter of pure contemplation, no problem of philosophy. It is vital, essential, fundamental, and demands immediate and full attention. It claims the careful consideration of every mind, conscience, heart, and will.

It is not a matter of mere argument, still less of personal indifference what a man thinks of Jesus Christ. There are those who seem to think that so long as the spirit and life are right, opinion counts for very little. This was not Christ's own view. He regarded it as of importance that men should have right opinions about Him. "Who do men say that I am?" He was above all things solicitous of training His disciples in the direction of right thoughts of Himself. There are, of course, many things in life on which we may have an open mind, and in which right opinion or wrong opinion leads to no serious results, but this is not the case in regard to Christ, for it does matter very much what we think of Him and what our attitude to Him is. What we receive from Christ will largely depend on what we believe Him to be. It is obvious that the results must necessarily be vastly different according as we regard Christ as a good man or as God manifest in the flesh. Everything we know of God, and everything we need from Him, is deeply affected by our attitude to Christ. If He be not God then fellowship with Him is an impossibility, for He is dead "in the lorn Syrian town," and we cannot get into personal contact even with His writings, for He left none. So in regard to redemption from sin, it matters very much whether Christ is God, because our view of His death turns on this fact. If He were any one other than God His death would differ in no respect from an ordinary death. If He be not God, then God's gift of Him, and His love in giving, would be no giving Himself, and would have no special and unique characteristics. And even in regard to prayer and worship, if Christ be not God our approach to Him in prayer were nothing short of irreverence and blasphemy in placing Him where God alone should be. It makes a profound difference, therefore, what we think of Christ, for one cannot reasonably, honestly, and heartily trust, follow, and obey Christ if he has no definite and strong convictions as to His Deity.

Verification, therefore, is the great essential, the imperative necessity. We must verify the claim of Christ and come to some definite conclusion concerning Him. And it is to this that we now call attention.

What is the great, the supreme problem in connection with Christ? It is to discover how a historical personality can become a religious fact for all men. How can a historic Person who appeared at one point of time centuries ago become the permanent religious fact and force for all time? How can One who appeared under the specific conditions and limitations of history be the universal spiritual life of millions in all ages, races, and circumstances? There have been several attempts to solve this problem.

Many argue that the solution is found in reverting to the historical Christ of the Gospels, in discovering the essential features of "the inner life of Jesus," and making that the standard of our life. "Back to Christ" has been for years the watchword of a school of thinkers with the object of recovering and realising for to-day the personality of Jesus Christ. But does it really help faith and satisfy human needs to-day to revert to the past, to picture a Christ of centuries ago, and to live solely in the light of that great Figure? We need and must have something far more real, far more definite, far more *present* than this. The Christ who is to be our life to-day must be something more than a fact, however beautiful, of nineteen centuries ago.

People told us some years ago that our views of the Gospel were inadequate, and the direction was shouted to us—"Back to Christ!" Well, we went back: and we found that they had prepared the scenery and the dresses and the manners and customs of His Palestinian environment, and they told us about the subjects of His teaching, and gave us a syllabus of His method and His views upon religious questions, and they said, "Thus and thus spake the Teacher of Galilee: in this and that group of sayings we unfold to you the mind of the Master!" It is all very beautiful and valuable: it is always educative to be made conscious of the spaces of history, and to be reminded of facts and truths which have been unduly subordinated. But has there not been all the while at our hearts a chill—a loneliness? Is not the deepest religious question, after all, for each man, this: whether there be in Christ a present Saviour, who can cover *me* now with the robe of His righteousness? No historic research, no exposition of the doctrines of an old-world Teacher, removes the burden of the friendlessness of my sin-stained soul in a universe ruled by a holy God. If by your scholarship you so make to live again the classic scenes in which the Nazarene moved and taught that I am made painfully conscious of the long centuries that intervening divide Him from me: then all the more, if you would secure the abiding of my faith in Him, you must let me see how He can still reach *me*, and stand for *me*, the wings of His affluent personality outstretched to cover me.[1]

Others adopt a different method of solving the problem. They do not concern themselves with the Personality, but concentrate attention on His ideas. The real meaning and significance of Christ, on this view, lies in the principles which actuated Him, and which He taught His disciples. Love, self-sacrifice, pity, tenderness, right-

[1] Johnston Ross, *The Universality of Jesus*, pp. 15 ff.

eousness, holiness—these and many other similar ideas
are the essential things in life, and they are to be realised
and lived without concerning ourselves about the Personality in which they were originally embodied. But
the question at once arises whether this method meets
all the demands of the situation. It may suit the philosopher, but will it satisfy the needs of the average man?
There is such a thing as sin in the world and in the
human heart, and ideas, however lofty, have never yet
proved powerful enough to meet its terrible force. Let a
man endeavour to help a fellow-sinner in his need when
he comes with a burdened conscience and a haunting
past. Let a man work among the fallen, the degraded,
the vicious. Ideas will prove utterly powerless. Let a
man face his own sin, the plague of his own heart, and
try to get rid of it. Ideas will prove utterly futile and
leave him more hopeless than before. Ideas in Christ
were the expression and achievement of His Personality, and it is this difference of fact and experience between His life and ours that makes the burden and
condemnation of sin still more real. "Ideals may charm
the intellect, but cannot satisfy the heart."[1] If men
could be saved and blessed by ideas, then the disciples
of Christ after those wonderful three years of His teaching would surely have enjoyed the most uplifting and
transforming of experiences. But we know they were
morally powerless and entirely incapable of translating
those ideals into reality. Ideas have no moral dynamic,
and our deepest need is not knowledge, but power—a
power in life that makes for righteousness.

The only God that can reveal Himself to us is one who
shows Himself to us in our moral struggle as the Power to

[1] Quoted in Streatfield, *The Self-Interpretation of Christ*, p. 41.

which our souls are really subject. This is what is vouchsafed to us in the revelation of God in Jesus Christ.[1]

Yet again, others endeavour to solve the problem of Christ's historic Personality as a religious fact and force by laying all the stress on personal spiritual experience as something really independent of historical fact and criticism. It is argued that even if we knew little or nothing more than the fact of Christ's life on earth, we should still be able to experience His grace and power as a living personal Saviour and Friend. The experiences of Christian men in all ages would, it is said, be a sufficient certification and guarantee that given the same conditions of personal reception and appropriation, the same spiritual results would accrue. Now there is a profound truth in the emphasis placed by this view on spiritual experience, and the way in which it has been insisted on during recent years and the power with which it may be used in life can hardly be overestimated. It is one of our strongholds of certitude.

> "Whoso hath felt the Spirit of the Highest,
> Cannot confound, or doubt Him, or deny.
> Yea, with one voice, O world, though thou deniest
> Stand thou on that side, for on this am I."

But experience as the sole and adequate foundation for religious life is a very different matter, and those who take up this position really admit its inadequacy in being compelled to predicate some knowledge, however slight, of the historical fact of Christ's life on earth. Even the mere knowledge that He lived and died is a testimony to the need of some historic foundation. The Christ of Experience cannot be sundered from the Christ

---

[1] King, *The Seeming Unreality of the Spiritual Life*, p. 218.

of History, and the appeal to experience is impossible unless experience is based on historic fact. The history must guarantee the experience in the individual to-day just as the history has been the basis of the Church's experience in all ages. If we lose our faith in the historic fact of the Christ of the Gospels it will not be long before we lose our faith in the experience of the Christ of to-day. This process of disintegration is even now being realised among those who are reducing to virtual valuelessness the Gospel records of Jesus Christ. The Christ of faith cannot be separated from the Jesus of history without our soon losing both. If there is one thing that modern scholarship has made clear beyond question, it is that it is now impossible to deny that Jesus Christ had a unique relationship to God and a unique relationship to man, and it is this uniqueness that provides the foundation and must give the warrant for that experience of Christ to-day which every Christian has and enjoys. It is vain to think that by sublimating the history into a philosophy we can retain its reality and power. It is impossible even for the learned to possess for long the Spirit of Jesus if we surrender the historical Jesus, while the attempt to set aside the historical Jesus in the case of ordinary people would result in the loss of vital Christianity altogether.

What, then, is the true solution of this all-important problem? There is essential truth in all the foregoing contentions, but none of them singly is anything like the whole truth. The solution is found in taking the truths in all these three suggested solutions, and uniting them and making them effective for life by means of that which is the unique feature of Christianity as a Divine revelation. What this is will be evident from an incident. Some time ago a thoughtful French pastor

expressed to the writer great perplexity in the face of
the fact that while scholars often spent years in arriving
at adequate conclusions about the Jesus of the Gospels,
unlettered Christian people became convinced of the
reality of Jesus Christ through experience, with scarcely
any difficulty. He could not understand the reason for
these very different results. "May it not be due," he was
asked, "to the Holy Spirit?" "How so?" he replied, "the
Holy Spirit does not witness to a man's heart that Jesus
was born in Bethlehem, lived at Nazareth, worked in
Capernaum, and died in Jerusalem." "No," was the
answer, "but the Holy Spirit is admittedly the Spirit of
Truth, and the fact that He does witness to Jesus and
does make Him real to the soul, and that He does *not* do
this in regard to Mohammed, or Buddha, or Plato, is
surely a proof that the facts about Jesus are *true*, or the
Holy Spirit would not witness to them." "I never thought
of that," he said; "I believe this will resolve my difficulty."

Is it not in this way that the problem of the personality of Christ as a religious fact for to-day is to be solved?
Jesus Christ said of the Holy Spirit, "He shall glorify
Me, for He shall receive of Mine and shall shew it unto
you." Bishop Thirlwall once said that "the great
intellectual and religious struggle of our day turns mainly
on this question Whether there is a Holy Ghost." Observe how this works out. Historical criticism may send
us back to Christ, may insist on our concentrating attention on the Jesus of the Gospels, and may produce for
us what it regards as the true picture of that Personality. Then the Holy Spirit will take the irreducible
minimum which criticism has left, and has been compelled to leave simply because it is irreducible, and will
use it to impress, convince, and inspire the soul with its

picture of a unique, sinless, perfect, Divine Figure. In the same way the ideas which philosophy finds in such fulness and fruitfulness in the historic Jesus will be taken' by the Holy Spirit and made real and vital to the soul. For Christian life and character it is not possible to dwell much on mere ideals, for they are matters of philosophy rather than of religion. Ideals must be realised if they are to be of value for life, and the work of the Holy Spirit is to make these ideals of Christ real in the souls of His followers. It is for this reason that neither the Example of Christ nor His ideas are of special practical value if considered alone. *Imitatio Christi* is but a small part of the truth: *Repetitio Christi* is nearer the whole. Christ is not fully set before us when He is regarded simply as an external Object to imitate, and when His ideas and ideals are to be produced in us by imitation. The true life is that which comes as the result of the Holy Spirit glorifying Christ in the heart and working in us that life and those ideas.

And this has already brought us to the central truth of Christianity, that the Holy Spirit brings to bear on our hearts and lives the presence and power of the living Christ, and thereby links together the Christ of History and the Christ of Faith. The Holy Spirit, in a word, is God active in the soul for man's salvation, and the purpose and method of His activity is the revelation of Christ to heart and life. The Holy Spirit is thus no impersonal influence, but God Himself in contact with the spirit of man. In the abysmal deeps of personality He is at work, and what He does is simply this: He makes Christ *real* to the soul. And thus the work of the Holy Spirit in relation to Christ is the very heart of Christianity, and by means of it the antithesis between past and present, history and experience, objective and subjective, is, if not reconciled, at any rate transcended, and God and man meet in Christ for life and fellowship, character and conduct, holiness and service.

Christianity, in a word, meets and hallows our broadest views of nature and life. It receives the testimony of universal history to the adequacy of its essential teaching to meet the needs of men. It reaches with unfailing completeness to the depths of each individual soul. The Person of Christ includes all that belongs to the perfection of every man. The Spirit of Christ brings the prayer through which each one can reach his true end. Christianity, in a word, to sum up what has been said already, offers us an ideal and offers us strength to attain to it.[1]

We end, therefore, where we began, by saying that Christianity is Christ, and we add thereto the complement —Christ becomes Christianity for us by the Holy Spirit of God. In these two truths are found essential Christianity and the simple though sufficient secret of its verification and proof.

It follows, therefore, to present our conclusion under another aspect, that the ultimate criterion, the adequate verification, of Revelation to man, in its parts and in its completeness, lies in its proved fitness for furthering, and at last for accomplishing, his destiny. . . . This character belongs perfectly, as we affirm, to the Gospel. If it could be shown that there is one least Truth in things for which the Gospel finds no place; if it could be shown that there is one fragment of human experience with which it does not deal; then, with whatever pathetic regret it might be, we should confess that we can conceive something beyond it—that we still *look for another*. But I can see no such limitation, no such failure in the Gospel itself, whatever limitations and failures there may have been and may be still in man's interpretation of it. Christ in the fulness of His Person and of His Life is the Gospel. Christ in

[1] Westcott, *The Gospel of Life*, p. 110.

the fulness of His Person and of His Life is the confirmation of the Gospel from age to age.[1]

The crowning proof of the revelation of the Christ of the Gospels and of experience is that He is capable of being reproduced by the Holy Spirit in the lives of His followers. The culminating evidence of the Godhead of Christ is that He is able by the Holy Spirit to bestow His Divine life on the lives of all who are willing to receive Him. "As many as received Him, to them gave He power to become the sons of God, even to them that believe on His Name" (John i. 12). He thus assures us at once of the certainty of human access to God and of Divine approach to man. All other views of Christ fail either on one side or the other. A human Christ would be unable to satisfy us as to access to God, while a Christ who is not directly in touch with God could not assure us of any direct approach of God to man. Like Jacob's ladder, which was set up on earth with the top reaching to heaven, Jesus Christ in His human life is a solid foundation, and in His Divine life is a sure guarantee for every soul that wishes to come to God by Him and to commune with God through Him.

We see, then, that for human life Christ is essential, Christ is fundamental, Christ is all. We may, like some, reject Him. We may, like others, be impressed and attracted without definitely yielding to Him. Or we may be intellectually convinced and yet try to evade Him. But the one thing we cannot do is to ignore Him. "What think ye of Christ?" is a question that has to be answered. "What shall I do with Jesus?" is a question that cannot be avoided. The question is far too serious to be ignored even if we could do so. The remarkable

[1] Ibid., p. 112.

fact about Christ is that, unlike every other founder of religion, He cannot possibly be overlooked. Even the attempt to ignore Him is in reality a confession of an opinion about Him. Indifferentism is possible about many things, but absolutely impossible about Christ.

Christ's call to the soul is four-fold: Come unto Me, Learn of Me, Follow Me, Abide in Me. Come unto Me as Redeemer; Learn of Me as Teacher; Follow Me as Master; Abide in Me as Life. And all that is required of us is the one sufficient and inclusive attitude of soul which the New Testament knows as faith (πιστεύειν εἰς). This attitude and response of trust, self-surrender, dependence, is the essential attitude and response of the soul of man to God. Every sincere man knows full well the impossibility of realising his true life in isolation, apart from God. Faith as man's response to God for ever puts an end to the spiritual helplessness and hopelessness of the solitary man. It introduces him to a new relationship to God in Christ, and opens the door to the coming of the Holy Spirit of light and life. It is the means whereby the needed strength, satisfaction, and security come to the soul from fellowship with God. Faith introduces the soul into a new world of blessed fellowship, uplifting motives, satisfying experiences, and spiritual powers, and from the moment the attitude of trust is taken up the Holy Spirit begins His work of revealing Jesus Christ to the soul. He brings into the heart the assurance of forgiveness and deliverance from the burden of the past, He bestows on the soul the gift of the Divine life, and then He commences a work that is never finished in this life of assimilating our lives to that of Christ, working in us that Christlikeness which is the essential and unique element of the Gospel ethic. In the deep and dim recesses of our personality the

Holy Spirit works His blessed and marvellous way, transfiguring character, uplifting ideals, inspiring hopes, creating joys, and providing perfect satisfaction. And as we continue to maintain and deepen the attitude of faith the Holy Spirit is enabled to do His work and we are enabled to receive more of His grace. "That we might receive the promise of the Spirit through *faith*" (Gal. iii. 14). By every act of trust and self-surrender we receive ever larger measures of the life of Christ, and all the while we are being changed into the image of Christ "from glory to glory" by the Spirit of the Lord.

IMMORTAL love, for ever full,
    For ever flowing free,
For ever shared, for ever whole,
    A never-ebbing sea.

Our outward lips confess the Name
    All other names above;
Love only knoweth whence it came,
    And comprehendeth love.

We may not climb the heavenly steeps
    To bring the Lord Christ down;
In vain we search the lowest deeps,
    For Him no depths can drown.

And not for signs in heaven above
    Or earth below they look,
Who know with John His smile of love,
    With Peter His rebuke.

In joy of inward peace, or sense
    Of sorrow over sin,
He is His own best evidence—
    His witness is within.

No fable old, nor mythic lore,
  Nor dream of bards and seers,
No dead fact stranded on the shore
  Of the oblivious years;

But warm, sweet, tender, even yet
  A present help is He;
And faith has still its Olivet,
  And love its Galilee.

The healing of His seamless dress
  Is by our beds of pain;
We touch Him in life's throng and press
  And we are whole again.

O Lord and Master of us all,
  Whate'er our name or sign,
We own Thy sway, we hear Thy call,
  We test our lives by Thine.

Our thoughts lie open to Thy sight;
  And, naked to Thy glance,
Our secret sins are in the light
  Of Thy pure countenance.

Apart from Thee all gain is loss,
  All labour vainly done;
The solemn shadow of Thy Cross
  Is better than the sun.

Alone, O Love ineffable,
  Thy saving Name is given;
To turn aside from Thee is hell,
  To walk with Thee is heaven.

We faintly hear, we dimly see,
  In differing phrase we pray;
But, dim or clear, we own in Thee
  The Light, the Truth, the Way.

—Whittier

BIBLIOGRAPHY

Baillie, J. *Invitation to Pilgrimage*. 1942.
Box, G.H. *The Virgin Birth of Jesus*. 1916.
Box, G.H. Article "Virgin Birth," *Dictionary of Christ and the Gospels*. 1908.
Bruce, A.B. *The Miraculous Element in the Gospel*. 1893.
Bruce, A.B. *The Parabolic Teaching of Christ*. 1899.
Brunner, E. *Revelation and Reason*. 1947.
Brunner, E. *The Mediator*. 1934.
Cawley, F. *The Transcendence of Jesus Christ*. 1936.
Craig, S.G. *Christianity Rightly so Called*. 1947.
Curtis, J. *Jesus Christ the Teacher*. 1943.
Denney, J. *Jesus and the Gospel*. 1907.
Denney, J. *The Death of Christ*. 1911.
Denney, J. Article "Preaching Christ," *Dictionary of Christ and the Gospels*. 1908.
Dodd, C.H. *The Apostolic Preaching and its Development*. 1936.
Fairbairn, A.M. *The Place of Christ in Modern Theology*. 1893.
Fairbairn, A.M. *Studies in the Life of Christ*. 1907.
Flew, J.N. *Jesus and His Church*. 1935.
Forsyth, P.T. *The Person and Place of Jesus Christ*. Reprinted 1947.
Forsyth, P.T. *The Work of Christ*. Reprinted 1947.
Glover, T.R. *The Jesus of History*. 1917.
Gore, C. *The Deity of Christ*. 1922.
Gore, C. *Jesus of Nazareth*. 1929.
Grensted, L.W. *The Person of Christ*. 1933.
Headlam, A.C. *Life and Teaching of Jesus Christ*. 4th Edition, 1940.
Hoskyns, E. *The Riddle of the New Testament*. 1936.

Hunter, A.M. *The Unity of the New Testament.* 1943.
Lamont, D. *Christ and the World of Thought.* 1935.
Lamont, D. *The Creative Work of Jesus.* 1924.
Lewis, C.S. *Miracles.* 1947.
Lewis, C.S. *The Screwtape Letters.* 1942.
Liddon, H.P. *The Divinity of our Lord.* 1866.
Machen, J. *Christianity and Liberalism.* 1929.
Machen, J. *Christian Faith in the Modern World.* 1936.
Machen, J. *The Virgin Birth.* 1933.
Mackay, J. *Preface to Theology.* 1942.
Manson, T.W. *The Teaching of Jesus.* 1931.
Manson, W. *Jesus the Messiah.* 1943.
Moffatt, J. *Jesus Christ the Same.* 1942.
Morgan, G.C. *The Crises of the Christ.* 1905.
Morgan, G.C. *The Teaching of Christ.* 1913.
Morrison, F. *Who Moved the Stone?* 1930.
Mullins, E.Y. *Christianity at the Crossroads.* 1924.
Neill, S. *Foundation Beliefs.* 1941.
Nunn, H.P.V. *What is Modernism?* 1932.
Orr, J. *The Christian View of God and the World.* 1902.
Orr, J. *The Virgin Birth of Christ.* 1908.
Orr, J. *The Resurrection of Jesus.* 1908.
Orr, J. Article "Jesus Christ," *International Standard Bible Encyclopedia.* 1923.
Ramsay, A.M. *The Resurrection of Christ.* 1945.
Rawlinson, A.E.J. *Christ in the Gospels.* 1944.
Richardson, A. *The Miracle Stories of the Gospel.* 1941.
Scroggie, W.G. *Christ in the Creed.* 1928.
Simpson, P.C. *The Fact of Christ.* 1900.
Smyth, J.P. *A People's Life of Christ.* 1921.
Stalker, J. *The Christology of Christ.* 1900.
Taylor, F.J. *The Church of God.* 1946.
Taylor, V. *Forgiveness and Reconciliation.* 1941.
Temple, W. *Christus Veritatus.* 1939.
Warfield, B.B. *Biblical Doctrines.* 1929.
Warfield, B.B. *The Lord of Glory.* 1907.